Ancient Astronauts

Those Who From Heaven Came To Earth

"The resistance to a new idea is increased
by the square root of it's importance"

- Jason Martell

Table of Contents

Introduction by Jason Martell

All ancient cultures speak of a time when they had connections with beings not from Earth that were both spiritually and technologically more advanced than us. Yet in modern times, we have still not managed to make contact with extraterrestrial life. I often wonder why this disconnection with more advanced beings has taken place. What is more, I wonder how their existence can be discounted in the face of the evidence they have left of themselves and their culture in literally every corner of our planet.

How did we get here? Where did we begin? Who created us? Throughout human history, our religious traditions have asserted many—often conflicting—explanations for these questions. Similarly, scientists and historians have put forth countless theories and analyses of antiquity. All too often, religion and science come into direct conflict on these questions—with disastrous results. We can all call to mind examples of suffering, persecution and cruelty that have plagued our history as a result of conflicting viewpoints on our origins. Surely, such senseless and destructive conflict doesn't have to go on forever. But how can we ever expect to change as a race if we don't accept our place in the universe? Can we lift the veil that covers our eyes?

In this book, I will provide an easy and understandable gateway for introducing newcomers to the ancient astronaut theory and the true nature of our human history. Many people have a hard time conveying the impact this information has had on their lives. It is, in the truest sense, an apocalypse of knowledge—a revelation.

Their impact on our lives is reflected in the information gathered in this book. A visit by an extraterrestrial race would show all humanity that we are not alone and never have been. This would have dramatic affects on world religion and how we perceive our place in the universe. It is my sincere hope that, within our lifetime, we can make enough change and progress to be welcomed into the galactic inner circle as respected members.

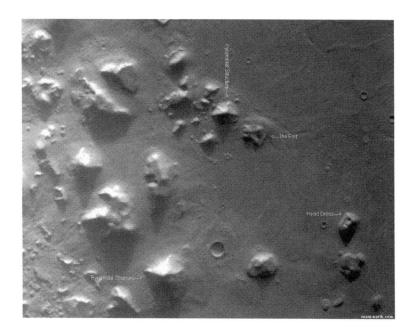

Structures On Mars

In 1996, I was attending college in San Diego, California. One day, someone tangentially mentioned to me that there were a "face" and "pyramids" on the surface of Mars. And that NASA had taken photographs of these objects.

Of course, I was very skeptical of this information and did not think much of it. It is common knowledge that the atmosphere of Mars is inhospitable to multicellular life forms —the only kind of life form that would be capable of constructing something artificial like this supposed "face" and these "pyramids." Surely, if NASA had taken pictures of artificial structures on the surface of another planet, this would be the biggest discovery of our lifetime. Yet this was the first time I had heard of Cydonia, the region of Mars where the Face and Pyramids are located, and the NASA photographs had been taken in 1976—twenty years earlier. Since I had never seen this topic covered on MSNBC or CNN, I assumed it must be ludicrous.

When I looked at the photos of the Face and Pyramids on Mars, they seemed remarkably similar to something I had seen here on Earth —the Sphinx and the Pyramids in Egypt. I had just started to learn how to use the internet in

1996, so I began to curiously look into what NASA and other sub-contracted agencies of NASA were currently studying. It turned out that the cameras attached to the orbiters we send to Mars are controlled by a company also located in San Diego, California—Malin Space Science Systems.

I contacted Dr. Malin, the scientist in charge of these operations, to ask him about the Face and Pyramids on Mars and he was kind enough to respond to me directly. He stated, "There is no evidence that the face and pyramids are artificial structures. We simply attribute them to sand and natural weather erosion." I found this answer really intriguing. Looking at the Cydonia region of Mars myself, it seemed incredibly clear that the Face, Pyramids, and even other surrounding objects must have been formed in some "artificial" way. The idea that these structures had come about merely through natural movements of wind and sand seemed akin to supposing that the presidential faces carved into Mount Rushmore were created by chance. Or—to suggest an even more relevant parallel—that the Great Sphinx of Giza was not the product of deliberate labor, but had simply emerged due to erosion.

I began to look for answers outside of NASA. I wanted to see who else was aware of these photographs of the Cydonia region and if any proper science had been done to explore whether these could possibly be artificial structures. I was able to find 5 to 10 peer level review scientists with PhD's in image analysis of satellite telemetry who were also studying these images. These were people who did not work for NASA, but had the same level of education and experience as NASA scientists.

One of these people is Dr. Mark Carlotto, an expert in satellite remote sensing and digital image processing. He had used mathematical algorithms to detect Russian military troops and artillery from satellite telemetry over Russia. Running these algorithms on Russian satellite telemetry showed that objects hidden by tarps or bushes still had a high probability of being artificial. Dr. Carlotto used these same mathematical algorithms on the satellite telemetry from the surface of Mars and found the Face and Pyramids to have over a 98% probability of being artificial. Dr. Carlotto began his work with the Face by applying a computer-vision technique called "shape-from-shading," which derived a 3-dimensional shape of the Face from the available Viking images. He then used computer graphics to create synthetic views of the Face from various perspectives and under differing lighting conditions. The results of these studies were positive, but when Carlotto submitted them in a paper to *Icarus* journal, they were rejected on the grounds that the Face itself was of "no scientific interest." The paper was ultimately published in the journal of *Applied Optics* in 1998.

It seems that mainstream science had dismissed the Face as being of any scientific relevance on the grounds that it was a purely accidental structure—that it was, in other words, naturally occurring and therefore of no possible interest. Carlotto began to develop objective methods to distinguish the face from other forms nearby. He wanted to show that it could potentially be artificial, rather than natural, in which case it would be of supreme interest. He began to concentrate on whether he could show the Face to be quantitatively different from the surrounding terrain.

Through a colleague, Carlotto learned about a recently developed algorithm, or computer routine, based on fractal mathematics. This algorithm was capable of identifying man-made objects—as distinct from naturally occurring objects—in aerial and satellite photographs. When applied to the Viking photos of the Face on Mars, the algorithm showed the Face to be the least fractal object —and therefore the least natural object—in the entire region. The algorithm also pointed to similar evidence of artificiality in the pyramidal objects near the Face. When Carlotto and his colleague Michael Stein submitted these results in their paper, "A Method for Searching for Artificial Objects on Planetary Surfaces," to the scientific journal *Nature*, it was rejected on the basis—once again!—that it was of "no scientific interest." Fortunately, the paper was published in 1990 in the *Journal of the British Interplanetary Society*.

What amazes me is that NASA never applied any level of scientific scrutiny to these structures. They just quickly dismissed these objects as just a trick of light and shadow. However, we found that statement to be erroneous.

The first image NASA took of the Face on Mars was back in the 70's from their Viking Orbiter. When the image was beamed back to NASA headquarters, they quickly labeled the shot "Head" and said that they re-imaged the same location several hours later and the face was gone. WRONG ANSWER NASA!

It turns out that NASA had taken several images of the "Head" from different orbital latitudes where the degree of the camera and the angle of the sun were different. And each time the face still is visible. It's a 3-

dimensional model carved in stone! Notice that the shadow on the face in the images below is different in each image, but it still looks like a face every time.

Skeptics suggest that we see the Face on Mars because we want to see it. Perhaps it does, to some degree, express our longing to know that we are not alone in the universe. Suppose, then, for the sake of argument, that the Face is just an optical illusion, some trick of the light as it plays across a naturally eroded Martian surface? Suppose we see these clear, symmetrical facial features because we are projecting our humanity out there into the galaxy from a desire to connect? If the Face is there purely by chance, what about all the other structures nearby? Structures that consistently express the same kind of high-level geometry?

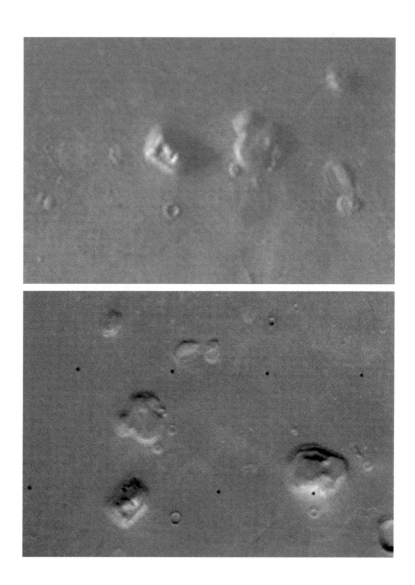

Dr. Tobias Owen, who is now professor of astronomy at the University of Hawaii, identified the Face on Mars on Viking frame 35A72. The same frame, covering approximately 34 by 31 miles - also shows many other features that could be artificial. These cluster around latitude 40 degrees north in the region of Mars known to astronomers as Cydonia, and were photographed from an altitude of more than 1,000 miles with relatively poor resolution.

These images above were located in the 1980's by researchers Vincent DiPietro and Gregory Molenaar, engineers at the Goddard Spaceflight Center. They did further studies on the large pyramidal object near the Face, which is approximately 500 meters high and nearly 3 kilometers in length. Now known as the D&M Pyramid after its discoverers, this structure expresses sophisticated geometry similar to other structures in the area. This has been confirmed by several other independent researchers.

Among the scientists who expounded upon the findings of DiPietro and Molenaar is Richard Hoagland, a former NASA consultant and archaeoastronomer who had originally accepted NASA's dismissal of the Face without question. It the early 1980s, however, he began to take a closer look. Hoagland discovered the group of pyramid-shaped mounds to the southwest of the Face—now termed the City. He also discovered a surprising structure consisting of very straight walls and open area in the center. This structure is now known as the Fort, for its shape clearly suggests that purpose. Going beyond the landform analysis techniques that had already been applied, Hoagland mathematically examined the spatial relationships of the various features and their relations to one another. He commissioned an analogue clay model of the region which, when held up to the computer studies, rendered a high degree of correlation. Hoagland's calculations clearly suggest the presence of a deliberate hand in the construction of these objects.

A casual glance at the image of the Cydonia region reveals only a jumble of hills, craters and escarpments. Gradually, however, as though a veil is being lifted, the blurred scene begins to feel organized and structured - too intelligent to be the result of random natural processes. Although the scale is grander, it looks the way some archaeological sites on Earth might look if photographed from 1,000 miles up. The more closely you examine it, the more it is apparent that it really could be an ensemble of enormous ruined monuments on the surface of Mars.

The same is also true for the D&M Pyramid, which I mentioned earlier. This five-sided structure stands about ten miles from the Face and, like the Great Pyramid of Egypt, is aligned virtually north south towards the spin axis of the planet. Its shortest side is a mile, its long axis extends to almost two miles and it is half a mile high. Commenting on the proximity of the Face and the D&M Pyramid, Richard Hoagland asks a pointed question: 'What are the odds against two terrestrial-like monuments on such an alien planet and in essentially the same location?'

Let's take a moment here to look a bit deeper into the geometry of the D&M Pyramid. For the following mathematical research, I wish to acknowledge the collaboration of the above mentioned Richard Hoagland.

D&M Pyramid Geometry

The D&M Pyramid appears to be positioned with architectural alignment to other enigmatic objects nearby that have also been studied as possibly artificial. The main axis of the D&M, as illustrated below, points at the Face in Cydonia. Henceforth we will refer to this direction as the "front" of the pyramid.

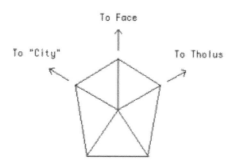

The front of the D&M Pyramid has three edges, spaced 60 degrees apart. As noted above, the center axis points to the Face. The edge on the left of this axis points toward the center of a feature that has been nicknamed the "City" by the Cydonia investigators. The edge on the right of the center axis points toward the apex of a dome-like structure known as the "Tholus." The five-sidedness, bilateral symmetry, and primary alignments were first observed by Richard Hoagland after studying quality digital enlargements prepared in 1984 by SRI International from negatives of images processed by DiPietro and Molenaar.

Turning back to the reconstructed geometry, we will now consider the internal symmetries of this object. The D&M Pyramid displays a complex interplay between five-fold and six-fold symmetry. Both symmetries are present simultaneously, with the front of the pyramid exhibiting six-fold symmetry, and the "ground level" of the pyramid yielding a 36 degree angle that is characteristic of five-fold symmetry.

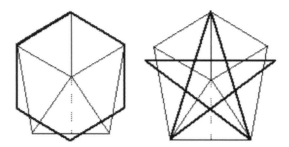

It is important to note that the practice of combining symmetries was widely practiced by the architects of antiquity. It was believed that geometry and certain mathematical relationships were crucial building blocks of the Cosmos, and that architecture should reflect these symmetries. These practices were later revived in the Islamic world and especially in Renaissance Europe. The angles formed by the D&M Pyramid when viewed from above differ from each other. Consequently, they can form various ratios. These angle ratios were studied to see if the values were significant, or merely random. The angle ratios display significant values, with a preponderance of square roots and fractions involving square roots. Once again, we have a theme used by Classical architects, who used the square roots of two, three, and five in laying out the proportions of their buildings. For clarity, three of these angle ratios are illustrated below:

Examples of Angle Ratios

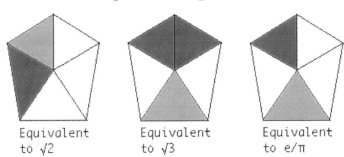

Equivalent
to √2

Equivalent
to √3

Equivalent
to e/π

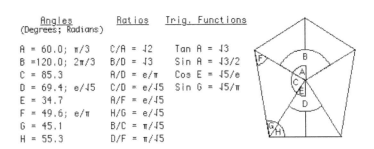

Angles (Degrees; Radians)	Ratios	Trig. Functions
A = 60.0; π/3	C/A = √2	Tan A = √3
B =120.0; 2π/3	B/D = √3	Sin A = √3/2
C = 85.3	A/D = e/π	Cos E = √5/e
D = 69.4; e/√5	C/D = e/√5	Sin G = √5/π
E = 34.7	A/F = e/√5	
F = 49.6; e/π	H/G = e/√5	
G = 45.1	B/C = π/√5	
H = 55.3	D/F = π/√5	

The ratios of the shaded angles are equivalent to the indicated values. In the above illustration, the ratio of the shaded angles is equivalent to the ratio of e (the base of the natural logarithms) and pi (the relationship between a circle's diameter and its circumference).

It should be noted that this ratio of *e/pi* is so nearly equal to the square root of three divided by two that it is insufficient to distinguish between these two possible values. Below is a table of the measured angles, and the results of the analysis. As you can see, the square roots of three and five, and the values of *e* and *pi* predominate. The identity of these values is strengthened by the numerous combinations in which they occur. Note that the radian measure and trigonometric functions of some angles yield the same values produced by the angle ratios. The geometry clearly has a common contextual thread.

It is important to remember that all of this geometry is "dimensionless." That is, this geometry is not dependent on such cultural conventions as counting by tens, or measuring angles in the 360 system.

Effectively, this geometry will "work" in any number system.

What can we conclude from this? The D&M Pyramid demonstrates a process of formation that is inconsistent with the surrounding geology. The natural geo-morphological processes observed on Mars fail to provide a potential mechanism for the D&M Pyramid's formation. More than that, they actually seem to preclude its very existence. Analysis of the Pyramid's geometry, and its alignment with other anomalous landforms, reveal intricate relationships that are numerous and logical, and are suggestive of highly sophisticated design. They clearly do not suggest random geological accident of formation.

This object has been compared with the elaborate symbolic architecture of antiquity. While much of the geometry is the same utilized by Classical architects, it is important to note that the implementation is totally different. Nowhere in Earth history is this exact type of geometric symbolism to be found. The same techniques used for most of this century in air photo interpretation show that the D&M Pyramid may be artificial, or may be a natural landform modified by intelligence. Either way, the balance of evidence suggests the presence of an intelligent, deliberate hand over the possibility of sheer chance.

Back to the Face

I become very fascinated with the Face and wanted to know for myself whether this structure was man made. I downloaded every high-resolution image of the face I could get from NASA going back to the 70's Viking missions.

In looking at the Face closely under magnification on a computer, I started to notice actual facial characteristics that I could recognize such as a nose, eyes, teeth and even a head dress of some sort that could be a helmet or head ornament. How could such details be so clear and have come about by accident?

I started to ask myself, "How could this be? Why is it that not one of my friends or anyone I know is aware of this?"

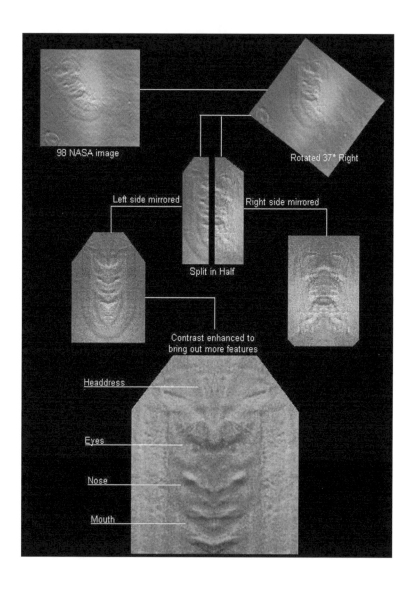

98 NASA image

Rotated 37° Right

Left side mirrored

Right side mirrored

Split in Half

Contrast enhanced to
bring out more features

Headdress

Eyes

Nose

Mouth

It seemed the face was badly eroded on the right side, but the left side still had very clear facial features. Knowing that all faces are asymmetrical, I decided to run a few tests on the face.

When you look at your face in a mirror, only exposing half your face, you still see your face in the mirror. The reflected side of your face matches the part not shown in the mirror. Applying this same practice to the Face on Mars brings out some interesting details.

Over the last 30 years, NASA has captured several images of the Face. For this test, I chose some of the more recent images shot in the 90's. It is interesting to note that the Face actually looks worse in more recent images. You would think that with improved camera technology, NASA would be able to produce clearer images of the Face over time. Yet, for some reason, the clearest images of the Face are from the 70's. Is NASA trying to hide something?

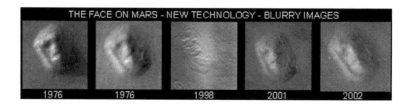

Back to the test....Taking the image you see here and mirroring the "left" and "right" side of the image produces some interesting results.

Looking at the right side, which is more eroded than the left, you can still see clear facial characteristics like eyes, nose, and mouth. There is an overall symmetry in its appearance. Next, look at the mirrored left half, which is not as eroded and shows much clearer features. Now we begin to see the real detail. Even the outer lining of the head seems to have a strong resemblance to a head dress.

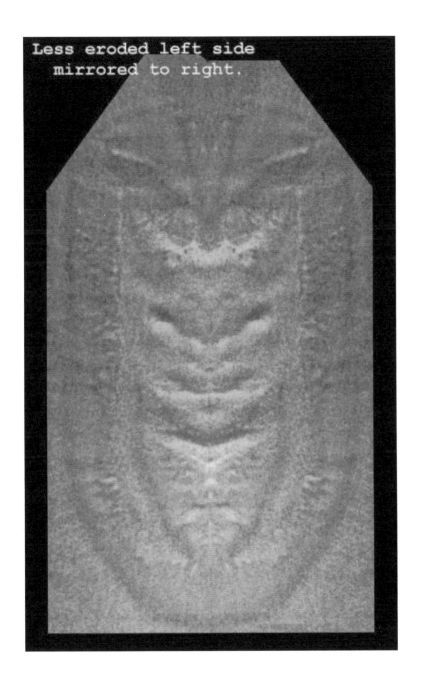

Less eroded left side mirrored to right.

29

The Face on Mars has now passed each test of artificiality yet proposed. These tests include a three dimensional structure, a lack of fractal patterns in the image, non-random distribution of the nearby small mounds, proximity of other anomalous landforms, an apparent bilateral symmetry, its location on the martian equator, having a culturally significant orientation, and serving an apparent culturally significant purpose.

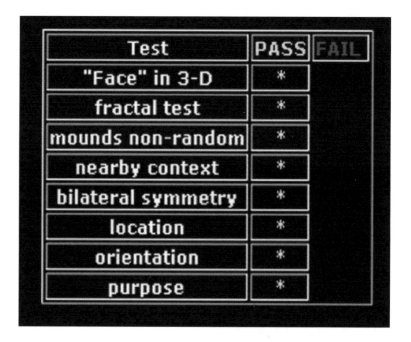

Test	PASS	FAIL
"Face" in 3-D	*	
fractal test	*	
mounds non-random	*	
nearby context	*	
bilateral symmetry	*	
location	*	
orientation	*	
purpose	*	

What do I mean by the importance of location, orientation, and cultural significance? Thinking back to our analysis of the D&M Pyramid, let's not forget that this structure stands only ten miles from the Face and, just like the Great Pyramid of Giza in Egypt, is aligned north-south towards the spin axis of the planet. As I mentioned earlier, its shortest side is a mile long, its longer axis is two miles and the whole thing is half a mile high. It is much bigger than any Pyramid here on Earth, but it is constructed in a clearly significant location and proximity to the Face —so strikingly similar to the Sphinx in Egypt and its geographical relation to the Great Pyramid. How could it be merely the product of random chance that two structures so similar to structures found in similarly co-ordinated locations here on earth could be entirely un-related? Clearly, there is some kind of connection between the two.

It would be an exaggeration to say that the case for artificiality is now compelling, and many thoughtful people will still find that conclusion less likely than all these "coincidences" put together. Yet the balance of the evidence, considered objectively, now weighs clearly in favor of artificiality over a natural origin of the Cydonian landforms.

Mars-Earth Connection

I started to reflect back on Egypt, with its famous Sphinx and Great Pyramids. The limestone Sphinx of Giza, with its massive human face crowned by an elaborate headdress, struck me as uncommonly similar to the Face on Mars. Not only that, both the Sphinx and the Mars Face are located in close proximity to massive Pyramids. Could this be mere random chance? There has to be a connection, a Mars-Earth connection.

The more I thought about what it might mean that there is a Face and Pyramids on Mars, the more I began to think about all the megalithic structures here on Earth. We have large stone monuments that are located on every continent, yet we don't really know for sure who built them and for what purpose. A perfect example is the Giza Pyramids.

According to mainstream science, the Egyptian Pyramids were constructed over a century and a half period from approximately

2630 to 2490 BC. The largest of the Pyramids, located near the Sphinx on the Giza plateau, is generally dated circa 2550 BC. Standing 147 meters high, it was the tallest monument in the entire world until the 19th century. The Great Giza Pyramid consists of nearly two and a half million stone blocks, each weighing from 2.5 to 15 tons. Scientists estimate that these massive blocks would have to have been set at a rate of one every two and a half minutes. What kind of work force could have been capable of such an impressive feat given the technology of the time?

If you ask an Egyptologist "Who built the Pyramids?" they will answer that ancient Egyptian workers devoted to their pharaohs built them. They base this theory on wall carvings and hieroglyphs depicting workers moving large blocks of stone.

But the real question should be "Where are the tools they used?" Large quarry sites from today use very large machinery to accomplish these monumental kinds of tasks. Where are the machines or advanced tools the ancient Egyptians used? The Great Giza Pyramid stands at the center of an extremely elaborate complex including many smaller pyramids, temples and several tombs. It is not enough to say that 20,000 people working 80 years straight could have built all of this WITHOUT the use of large quarry sites or tools to excavate the stones used.

New evidence has risen that raises even more questions as to the actual purpose of the Pyramids as well as their construction date. Using star mapping software on a PC, we can determine where the stars will be located at any specific time in the future or the past. This is useful for knowing that you can go outside your home at night and locate specific star constellations.

Using star mapping software over the Giza plateau reveals some interesting information about the three Pyramids and the Sphinx located there. It turns out that the three Pyramids of Giza form a terrestrial map of the Orion constellation, as Orion would have appeared in 10,500 BC. Also, on that exact date, the Sphinx (a creature with the face of a human and the body of a lion) gazes east directly into the constellation of LEO, the lion.

Is this just coincidence? How could the Egyptians from 2,500 BC build the Giza Pyramids to precisely match the Orion Constellation from the year 10,500 BC?

It is certain that the principal Giza monuments form an accurate terrestrial map of the three stars of Orion's belt as these constellations appeared in 10,500 BC. Who could have been observing the skies over Giza in 10,500 BC and who, at that date, could have had the technical capacity to realize such monumental works as the Sphinx and the Pyramids? Egyptologists assert that there were no civilizations on Earth at that time, let alone one capable of planning and building such immense, well-engineered structures.

If they are right, why do the alignments of Giza so plainly and repetitively mirror the skies of the 11th millennium BC? There may be a 'terrestrial connection' between Giza and

Cydonia - the region of Mars where the mysterious structures are located - perhaps a common source that imparted the same legacy of knowledge and symbolism on both worlds.

If the structures are intelligently created, then what is their purpose? When you look closely at the image below, you can clearly see what appears to be a terrain difference right at about where a shoreline would be if the city were on the edge of land. The Face is positioned in a way that would be visible from the city. So are other key features in this area, like the D&M pyramid.

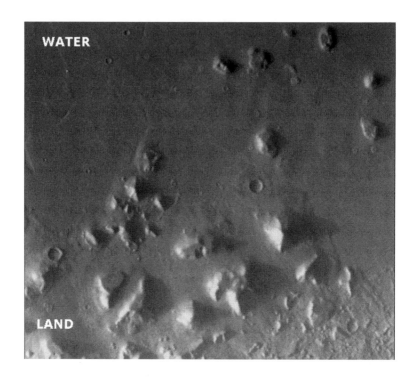

WATER

LAND

Is this just coincidence? NOPE. The geology alone speaks for its self. Whether or not the surface difference is caused by water, I am not able to say since I am not a geologist. But, in my opinion just by looking at the image myself, and the anomalies in the region, it seems quite possible that Cydonia was built right at the edge of water. On Earth, this is where we commonly build waterfront property.

The Giza Sphinx, too, stands on the west bank of the Nile River. Notice the color difference and the knobby terrain near all the pyramidal structures in the Cydonia region. These characteristics might well indicate that the pyramids were located on land. The Face, however, is surrounded by less knobby, lighter color surface.

The Sphinx is said to have been constructed between 2558 and 2532 BC. There is strong geological evidence that the Sphinx has been heavily weathered by water sometime in its past. The nature of the weathering suggests that it was caused by heavy rain over a long period of time. If the Sphinx was, in fact, built circa 2500 BC, as mainstream scientists claim, that would place its construction long after the climate changes that transformed Egypt into an arid landscape. When was the last time it rained on the Giza dessert? Just over 10,000 years ago…

Green on Mars?

It would be easy to take it for granted that the atmosphere of Mars is inhospitable to sustaining life. In fact, this is generally considered to be the case—which is a good reason why NASA would be so quick to dismiss the images of the Face on Mars and the Pyramids as mere natural by-products of wind erosion. To consider that these structures were deliberately created, we have to assume that the Martian atmosphere at some point was capable of supporting life. Currently, there is a vast body of evidence emerging that suggests that this may well have been the case at some time in the past.

Primarily, scientists have been examining what is known as the Gusev crater, a huge crater with a diameter of about 160 kilometers (90 miles). Many believe that the crater at one point was filled with water. The size and dimensions of the crater suggest that possibly a lake once stood there.

The NASA Spirit Rover landed in center of the Gusev crater in 2004. Images taken from the Rover's panoramic camera also show a number of interesting rocks. One rock outcropping, called the "Pot of Gold," has been thus named for its strange collection of nodules. There is also a cluster of rocks that resemble rotting loaves of bread and have therefore been dubbed the "Rotten Rocks."

The Mars Express spacecraft has gathered some other remarkable information. The mission of this spacecraft was initially to analyze in detail the chemical composition of the Martian atmosphere. The atmosphere on Mars consists of 95% carbon dioxide in addition to 5% other constituents which are not entirely known. Scientists suspected that this 5% is made up of a combination water, carbon monoxide, oxygen, formaldehyde and methane. The Mars Express was equipped with an instrument known as a Planetary Fourier Spectrometer (PFS), which is able to detect very specific molecules through an analysis of the molecule's light absorption mode. This is known as the molecule's "spectral fingerprint." This instrument was able to determine for certain that methane is present in the atmosphere of Mars. The next question is, where does it come from?

Unless there is a consistent source producing the methane that continually puts it out into the atmosphere, then the methane would only survive in the atmosphere for a few hundred years. This is because it oxidizes into water and carbon dioxide fairly quickly. Both water and carbon dioxide are present in the Martian atmosphere. However, since there is also still methane present, there must be some mechanism that puts it into the atmosphere on an ongoing basis.

One theory for the ongoing presence of methane involves the possibility of volcanic activity. However, so far no active volcanos have been detected on the surface of Mars. This makes it necessary to consider the other possibility—that the methane is a by-product of biological activity such as fermentation.

Taking this possibility into consideration, NASA's pictures of the Gusev crater using the Mars Global Surveyor, and the more recent Odyssey mission using the Themis Camera reveal some other interesting data as well. As you can see here, the images taken show a dark mass that at first glance seems to have characteristics that resemble some sort of plant life.

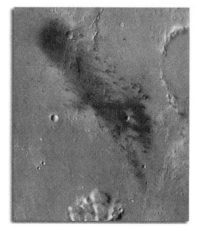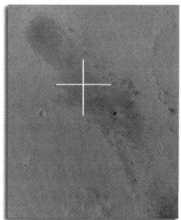

In 2004, the European Space Agency took its first full color image of the Gusev crater. What made the ESA image so immediately interesting was the "dark mass" features seen streaking in portions of the floor of the 90-mile-wide Crater in the NASA imaging (left). They can now be seen in true color by ESA revealed by Mars Express (right) to be various amazing shades of green.

At Gusev, if the craters in the area were indeed harboring conditions conducive to some special algae growth – primarily, by extending below the local water table -- then one could easily speculate that as the algae mats within some craters grow in the Martian spring and summer, and ultimately reproduce, their spores are carried by the winds out of the craters ... to form the long, sinuous streaks across the intercrater surfaces observed from orbit! The "streaks," then, would simply be more colonies of algae from the craters ... spread by algae spores surviving for a time between the crater floors.

However, deprived of crucial quantities of water and essential nutrients (which, in this scenario, would be concentrated on those crater floors), the migrating algae colonies between the craters quickly die ... and decompose. Through this process, they would inevitably release some of their bound organics – the hydrogen, carbon, etc. -- back into the atmosphere ... to be seen as significant quantities of methane gas.

During 2004 observations from the ESA Mars Express spacecraft in orbit around Mars, methane was detected in its atmosphere. And even more recently, methane has been detected on Mars by three independent groups of scientists. And this could be a sign of life-indicating, methane-producing bacteria.

In 2005, the "Pot of Gold" rock outcropping was examined in more detail. The Mars Spirit Rover discovered high concentrations of magnesium iron carbonate. This is a huge discovery. Carbonate originates only in wet, neutral conditions but dissolves in acidic conditions. Therefore, the presence of carbonate indicates that the ancient water which once pooled in the Gusev crater was not acidic. Rather, it was non-acidic water and therefore highly favorable habitat for supporting life. The substantial concentration of the carbonate deposit indicates a high probability that conditions were once highly conducive to supporting life in this place.

It becomes more and more clear that the Martian atmosphere has not always been so inhospitable to sustaining life. With this information, we must take into consideration the possibility that the remarkable Face and Pyramid formations on the surface of the planet did not simply emerge through natural processes. It becomes increasingly likely that their construction was deliberate at some point in the planet's long and mysterious history. If this is so, it begs us to consider the possibility of a connection between the Martian Face and Pyramids and certain remarkable constructions found on our own planet Earth…

Megalithic Structures All Over The Earth

I have briefly covered here a few of the characteristics around Giza that highlight evidence that Giza is much older than we thought. If this is true of the Giza Pyramids and the Sphinx, isn't it likely to be true of other ancient, megalithic structures? There are a baffling number of mysterious megaliths on this planet, and it makes sense to wonder if the mystery of their presence and construction is in some way connected. In this chapter, I will take you around the Earth, looking in detail at some of the world's most puzzling megalithic structures.

As I began my own studies of the megaliths, I wanted to know, "Where is the oldest civilization on earth? Where do we really come from?" Everyone has heard of the idea that there was once a great continent known as Atlantis. On this continent, there supposedly existed an advanced civilization, capable of complex mathematics, construction, and technology. Somehow, over many thousands of years, Atlantis was lost. It is impossible to determine what could have caused the disappearance of the Atlanteans. Some people claim that it sank into the ocean. As you will see later in this chapter, there are in fact a number of very puzzling ruins to be found underneath water at various points on the globe, including beneath Lake Titicaca in Bolivia and in Okinawa, Japan.

What if there was an advanced civilization at some point in the past around 10-15,000 years ago? Would they have simply stayed in one location and thrived? Or wouldn't they have been inspired to connect and colonize globally? Based on even an untrained observation of human history and behavior, we can suppose that a highly advanced civilization would not be content just to stay in one place. It seems far more likely that an advanced civilization would also be a global civilization, and we would see evidence of their technology all over the earth.

Some of the most recent data show hints that such a lost culture did exist. We can look at the discoveries of Kennewick Man, the red-haired mummies of Central Asia, the pale Ainu people of Japan, and the long faced stones of Easter Island for highly suggestive evidence. All of these discoveries feed into the mythology of the South American races who revered long-eared, light-skinned, bearded, elder gods from the heavens—deities who did not at all physically resemble themselves. At Nazca and we see the drawing of an "astronaut" who could not possibly have been meant to represent an indigenous person of the time period. In Tiahuanaco, a number of very strange looking 23-foot statues suggest the presence of another type of person besides the ancient people themselves.

Are these figures meant to represent "Gods"? They are often explained in this way. The long faces of Easter Island, the idols of Tiahuanaco —all are considered by mainstream scientists to be religious depictions, images of worship. Yes, it is highly likely that these ancient peoples would worship those who gave them the knowledge to build, to thrive, and to perform incredible feats of technological engineering. They would indeed have been gods to them.

If you asked the most ancient civilization, the Sumerians, about the source of their knowledge, they would say, "All we learned, we were taught by the Anunnaki." The word Anunnaki means "those who from heaven to earth came." It is easy to interpret this metaphorically, if we are approaching it from the standpoint that "heaven" is a mythical place. But what if it wasn't to them? What if it was a real place—the sky, outer space? What if, in fact, this arrival of god-like beings from the sky itself is the source material for our own Judeo-Christian concepts about a God that lives somewhere above us, somewhere off the Earth? We will discuss the term "Anunnaki" later in this book. You will see many references to them as likely candidates for the source of esoteric information.

If we look at Nazca, Stonehenge, Giza, Maccu Picchu, Teotihuacan, and many other megalithic locations around the world, we see evidence of monuments that are astronomically aligned with such precision it baffles modern scholars. There are numerous unexplained mysteries about the technology and mathematics that must have gone into the construction of many of these sites. Not only that, in several cases there is evidence that the civilization responsible must have had the power of flight, of an aerial viewpoint. There is no mainstream archaeological or

scientific theory that can explain many of
these facts taken alone, much less all of them
when considered together. We must look
deeper.

Baalbek

Lebanon's modern-day city of Baalbek was
known in ancient times as Heliopolis, or City
of the Sun. Through it ran a trade route
linking Damascus and Tyre. In the first century
AD, Roman engineers constructed a huge
complex of temples, dominated by the

Temple of Jupiter. This colossal structure is encircled by fifty-four towering columns. Including the Temple of Bacchus, this complex is an incredible feat of ancient engineering.

What is even more impressive than the complex itself, though, is what lies beneath it. This MASSIVE stone foundation covers more than five million square feet. Legend has it that the Sun god Helios landed upon the platform with his fire chariot. The site is also described in the ancient flood tale of Gilgamesh. This platform contains more stones than the Great Pyramid of Giza. There was no mortar used in constructing the platform, but it has not noticeably settled in thousands of years. This is due to the incredible engineering of the retaining wall that holds it up. It is composed of a "trilithon" (a Greek word meaning "three stones") made up of three of the world's largest sections of hewn stone—each as tall as a five story building and weighing over 600 tons.

With modern technology, it would take more than a week just to set up the crane required to move one of these blocks. What tools did these ancient peoples use to carve out these enormous slabs of rock? Not only that, the quarry from which the rocks must have come is over a mile away. We know this because an even larger slab was abandoned there after being cut. Called "the Monolith" because of its enormity, this 72-foot long slab weighs 1,050 tons and is the largest section of hewn rock on earth. Though the Monolith was abandoned, these other massive stones were moved somehow. What tools could have been used to transport them over a mile's distance? And where is the evidence of those remarkable tools now?

Stonehenge

Probably the most famous of megalithic sites, England's Stonehenge, stands alone on the Salisbury Plain, west of Amesbury. At first glance, the series of upright stones may seem shorter than expected. The tallest of the stones is 6.7 meters (22 feet) above ground—with another 2.5 meters (8 feet) buried below ground. It is the highly sophisticated arrangement of the stone settings that makes Stonehenge stand out from other prehistoric European monuments. These settings were constructed from two distinct types of stone: sarsen, a type of hard sandstone, and bluestone, a rock mixture found in the Preseli Mountains of Southwest Wales. It is not known how these bluestones reached the Salisbury Plain, but it was most certainly the result of determined effort involving both overland and oversea transport. But this is just one of the unanswered mysteries surrounding Stonehenge.

Though only 17 remain standing, the outermost ring of Stonehenge once consisted of 30 upright sarsen stones—each weighing approximately 25 tons. They were connected at the top by a chain of horizontal lintels. What is remarkable about the lintels is that not only are they joined together by simple mortise-and-tendon joints; they are also locked into place by a complex dovetail joint. All of the edges were smoothed into a remarkably graceful curve that followed the complete circle.

Recent evidence dates the site to approximately 8000 B.C. The stones are perfectly constructed for predicting and sighting a wide variety of astronomical alignments including the precession of the equinoxes. Mainstream science even acknowledges the astronomical significance of Stonehenge. But the truth is, no mainstream scientific theory has not really been able to explain the purpose of Stonehenge, nor exactly who built it—or how it was achieved. Surrounding the sarsen circle, there were originally a total of 60 standing bluestones with lintels. 60—the classic Anunnaki sexagesimal number, also embedded in our standard of time (60 seconds X 60 minutes=3600, the number of years in Nibiru's orbit).

The nearest possible source for the massive sarsen stones that comprise Stonehenge is the Marlborough Downs—18 miles to the Northeast. The heaviest of the sarsens weighs 45 tons. How did the mysterious builders of Stonehenge transport so many of these massive stones such a distance? The best theory mainstream science has to offer is that they used "some type of sledge." But what type of sledge and with how much manpower? And where are its remains?

Easter Island

An triangular slab of volcanic rock in the South Pacific, Easter Island is more than 2,000 miles from the population centers of Tahiti and Chili. It is one of the most isolated places on the face of the Earth. Dotting its coastline is a mysterious series of enormous carved stone heads known as the "Moai." Carved out of compressed volcanic ash, each of these monoliths weighs an average of 14 tons. No one knows how the ancient islanders could possibly have moved the Moai into their various positions around the island—miles from the location they were quarried.

Although some theorize that the faces of the Moai represent the spirits of the ancient islanders' ancestors or chiefs, there is no known written record to support this theory. There is in fact no evidence of their purpose at all. Not only that, the quarry from which the monoliths came raises more unanswered questions. Hundreds of half-finished monoliths lie there. What happened to interrupt the islanders' production of the Moai? Why were they building such a massive number of them in the first place? Some of the unfinished Moai weigh up to 165 tons! How were they going to transport something so massive?

Archaeologists attribute discovery of Easter Island to the Polynesians around the year 400 AD. They date the construction of the Easter Island monoliths between 1400 and 1600 AD. These early islanders, according to archaeological theory, also had the only written language in Oceania—the Rongorongo script. In addition, they left behind rock and woodcarvings and many elements of a rich culture that survive today, including crafts, tattooing, dance and music. Yet there is nothing to explain the Moai—no written record of how or why they were created, no cave wall drawings depicting their construction. Why would such a productive culture, in possession of a written language, utterly fail to document in any way an undertaking as massive as the construction and placement of the Moai? There is nothing to explain these monolithic mysteries.

Perhaps these monoliths radically pre-date the discovery of Easter Island by the Polynesians. Some suggest that the workers who "vandalized" the Anunnaki Nazca lines fled to Easter Island and constructed the Maoi with the techniques they learned from the Anunnaki.

Nazca

Etched upon the arid Peruvian coastal plain, 400 kilometers south of Lima, the Nazca lines are a series of elaborate geoglyphs depicting various types of creatures, plants, imaginary beings, and geometric shapes. They extend over an area of 450 square kilometers on the San Jose and Socos plains, and were discovered by chance in 1927—by an airplane pilot who happened to be flying over them. They are, in fact, so massive that they can only be seen from the air. This suggests, of course, that they were designed by a civilization capable of flight—a great mystery since they have been dated between 500 BC and 500 AD.

What figures do these lines depict? A great spider, a monkey, a dog, a lizard, a hummingbird, a condor, a whale, a fish—and what can only be described as an astronaut. This last figure clearly depicts a humanoid-shaped creature dressed in a puffy spacesuit. There's no way you can look at it without thinking that's what it is.

Why would an ancient civilization have depicted someone like this? Unless, of course, they had seen such a figure in real life. A visitor from a faraway land, whose knowledge and skill they chose to honor by carving his image into the earth.

Many suggest that the Nazca lines cover an area that would have made an ideal terminal —an ancient airport or spaceport. This is because it is one of the highest and driest places on earth—perfect for landing vehicles from above. Perhaps, too, its location and climate has made it possible for these lines to be preserved.

In addition to the animals and the astronaut—whose locations correspond to many major stars—there are a number of geometric diagrams and acute right triangles. These geometric forms clearly track the precession of the various constellations as they move across the night sky.

These lines were formed by a process of clearing and piling surface shale in a deliberate manner carefully designed to render these massive "drawings" only visible from the sky. Bits of pottery dated at 350 BC have been found among the shale. What civilization could possibly have had the power of flight at that date? And yet, it would have been impossible to know what they were drawing without being able to see it from far up in the sky.

It is generally acknowledged that the markings upon the plain were constructed in two separate phases. Many assume that "The Animal Phase" came first due to the fact that many of the animal pictograms have been obscured by later, more linear markings. This second series is referred to as "The Runway Phase" because it so clearly consists of triangular patterns and extremely long, continuous straight lines that resemble landing strips. It has been suggested that if there were indeed a lost civilization like Atlantis, they may have had good reason following global catastrophe to build landing strips of this nature. These landing strips might have been set up to facilitate escape from what was thought to be a doomed planet, or possibly to welcome refugees from other planets or colonies far away.

Whether or not this was the case, it is indisputable that many of the Nazca lines were designed and used as observations of astronomical cycles. They were first investigated by the German scientist Paul

Kosok, along with Peruvian archeologists Tello and Xesspe, who called them "the biggest astronomy book in the world."

Who were the people who made use of this massive astronomy book? And why?

Tiahuanaco

Let's turn now to Peru's neighbor, Bolivia. In the city of Tiahuanaco, 12 miles south of Lake Titicaca's southernmost tip, we find four remarkable ancient structures. One of these is known as Puma Punku, which I will discuss in greater detail in the next section. The other three are known as the Akapana Pyramid, the Kalasava Platform and the Subterranean Temple. The ruins of Tiahuanaco are often considered the oldest and the most inexplicable ruins upon the Earth. According to some, the wonder of their presence here surpasses the construction of the Egyptian Pyramids.

Tiahuanaco is located at an altitude of 13,300 feet—800 feet above the level of present-day Lake Titicaca. It is clear, however, that the city once must have been a thriving port built upon Lake Titicaca's shoreline. There is evidence of a brilliantly engineered waterworks system and an Anunnaki metal-smelting center here. This ancient Earth city is startlingly reminiscent of the Cydonia region of Mars—another Anunnaki site on the former shores of an ancient body of water.

It has been clearly established that the Tiahuanaco buildings cannot be attributed to the Incans, but that this once-great city was already in ruins when the Incans arrived. Bolivian archaeologist Arturo Posnansky has dated the Tiahuanaco pre-Incan culture at 1600 B.C. and believes that it flourished until 1200 A.D. There is, however, no written record of the culture nor has the mystery of its disappearance been solved.

The sculpture and style of stonework found in Tiahuanaco are remarkable for their uniqueness and complexity. Grouped together, there are a number of statues depicting figures that appear to be wearing helmets. Their eyes are square and they have rectangular mouths, suggesting a difference in appearance from the Andeans indigenous to the region. These "idols," as they are called, stand 23 feet high and many of them appear to have been cast somehow, rather than carved from the stone.

What was once the main temple of Tiahuanaco is known as the Kalasaya, a huge structure now in ruins. Its stone steps consist of a number of rectangular stone blocks, each

30 feet wide. The Kalasaysa was once dominated by one of the most compelling structures on the site—the Gate of the Sun. This is a huge monolithic structure, a gigantic doorway carved from a single block of stone that weighs 15 tons. Its upper portion is decorated by an extremely complex and detailed sculpture in bas-relief. The sculpture on the Sun Gate has been called a "calendar" and recognized as such since its discovery, as it obviously represents a solar year. It doesn't easily fit, though, into the solar year as we divide it in the present day. Many scientists and scholars have puzzled over it unsuccessfully, trying to figure out how to "read" it in modern terms. Eventually, it was declared simply a form of art, and dismissed as such.

Not everyone was comfortable with this dismissal, however. According to Professor Hans Schindler-Bellamy, a published and recognized scholar in this area, this elaborate bas-relief sculpture represents a special kind of calendar. Along with the American astronomer Dr. Peter Allan, Schindler-Bellamy spent years puzzling out the complexity of this calendar. Their findings were published in a book over 400 pages long, called The Calendar of Tiahuanaco. Their findings indicate that the calendar was designed for a particular purpose and time, and that it must reflect the events of that time—hence, it is impossible to force a translation. Instead, the calendar speaks for itself and those who made it. It is, in effect, a long and complex story, incorporating everything from the daily lives of the laborers to their advanced understanding of mathematics and astronomy.

From analysis of the calendar, it is clear that the ancient Tiahuanacans had determined long before the Egyptians the ratio of *pi*. They could also calculate squares and square roots, fractions, and angles based on sophisticated trigonometry. They knew how to render perfectly straight lines and precise right angles. Yet none of their mathematical instruments have been found.

It turns out that the solar year represented in the calendar is nearly the same as our own, but the earth must have revolved more quickly at that time, so their year was only 290 days long. It seems that at the time of Tiahuanaco's bustling civilization, the Earth's moon was not yet our companion but was still an independent planet. There was, however, another satellite that moved around the Earth, and it was closer, so that it moved around the Earth more quickly than our planet's rotation. It caused many solar eclipses, which are documented in the great calendar of the Gate of the Sun. The calendar also offers a wealth of precise astronomical information beyond this—including the beginning of the year and the days of the equinoxes and solstices, as well as the obliquity of the planet. It is clear that this ancient culture was perfectly aware that the Earth was round, and that it rotated on its axis rather than being flat with the sun moving over it. This is obvious because they have calculated and recorded into the calendar the exact times of solar eclipses not visible from Tiahuanaco—solar eclipses that must have occurred on the other side of the Earth.

This gives rise to numerous speculations, of course, including the question of how they were able to be aware of what was happening in the opposite hemisphere of the globe. Did they have complicated sailing vessels that would have gone that far? There is no record of them. Were there flying vessels possibly? Or were they aided by a more advanced civilization?

It is impossible to ignore the parallels between the mystery of the Sun Gate calendar and the other baffling phenomenon of ancient monolithic structures and the disappearances of complicated, advanced civilizations. Like the lines in the Nazca Plain, the mathematical brilliance of the Tiahuanacan constructions implies complex geometry and air travel devices utterly beyond the technology of the time.

There is just one other mystery about the Tiahuanaco site that we must address before moving onto the specifically puzzling Puma Punku. Thanks to Boero Rojo, we now know that far beneath the surface of Lake Titicaca lie a complex series of stone temples, stairways, and roads that remain submerged beneath the water. Scientists agree that Lake Titicaca has slowly receded from the edge of the Tiahuanaco ruins over the course of about 4,000 years. How, then, could so much architecture lie far beneath its surface? This can only mean that the underwater ruins are far, far older than the lake itself...

Puma Punku

Here we find a truly mind-boggling construction—the massive ruins of a collapsed building upon what appears to be the remains of a giant wharf. The ruins of Puma Punku are just one of four structures in the ancient city of Tiahuanaco, where Lake Titicaca once lapped upon the shores.

This four-part collapsed structure consists of a number of incredibly massive stones. One stone from the remnants of the pier has been weighed at 440 tons—that's equal to about 600 full-sized automobiles! Many of the other construction blocks commonly weigh between 100 and 150 tons. And where was the quarry from whence these incredibly huge stones came? Ten miles away, on the western shore of Lake Titicaca. There is absolutely no technology known to the ancients that could have possible moved these stones so far, much less known to the Andean people of

500 AD whose very simple reed boats have survived them. In fact, even with today's technology and far-advanced engineering, it would be impossible to build a structure like Puma Punku.

The mind-bending puzzle of Puma Punku hardly stops with the seemingly impossible size of the construction blocks themselves. Much more than that, it is the technology and engineering that clearly went into its highly complex construction. The ruins at Puma Punku, once four levels high, are remarkably constructed as an interlocking puzzle. The engineering and mathematics that went into this design boggles the mind. Each of the blocks has been carefully cut to interlock with its neighbor, and the whole thing fits together like a complicated puzzle—without the use of mortar. Another startling engineering technique used involves cutting stones at extremely precise angles so that one lies on top of another perfectly without any space in between. This indicates not only an advanced knowledge of stone cutting, but of descriptive geometry as well. The uniformity of the blocks suggests prefabrication and mass production, a high level of technology and organization. Yet, those who built this wonder have left behind absolutely no written record.

According to scientists and archeologists who have examined the stones that went into the construction of Puma Punku, none of these stones could have been cut using any known ancient techniques. The stones of Puma Punku consist of granite and diorite—the hardest stones in the world barring the diamond itself. In addition, the stones were very deliberately, delicately and finely cut— the cuts are perfectly straight. Each of the holes bored into the stones is flawlessly circular and each of equal depth. They must have been cut using diamond tools. But there is absolutely no evidence of such tools, nor is diamond likely to have existed in this region of the world.

If these ancients didn't—couldn't have—used diamonds to cut these stones, then what did they use? And where did they learn their technique? The ruins have been dated by mainstream science all the way back to 500 BC, possibly even earlier. How could these ancient peoples have managed such a feat with the limited technology of the time? Is it possible the knowledge came from somewhere else?

Maps have been discovered that lend support to the theory of assistance by an advanced civilization—one with the power of flight. The Piri Reis, dated 1513, and the Oronteus Finaeus, dated 1531, map the coastline of South America, many rivers, and some parts of Antarctica—none of which were presumably mapped until 1818. Both of these maps include such accurate portrayals of these areas, including specific landmarks, that it is highly unlikely that they were constructed without the benefit of an aerial viewpoint. Although these maps are dated from the 14th century AD, there are clear indications that they have been copied from other, older maps.

Who made these maps and how were they able to see these areas from the sky? And what happened to these people? There are theories that the technologically advanced civilization responsible for these wonders was wiped out by a massive flood around 12,000 years ago. However, the clear evidence of tools, bones, and other detritus among the flood alluvia suggests that a highly civilized people were present even before the flood. Not only that, carvings of bearded people who are clearly not Andean have also been discovered throughout the area—lending weight to the theory of another, non-indigenous, civilized presence.

Teotihuacán

Thirty miles north of Mexico City lay the ruins of an impressive ancient city. Teotihuacán, The City of the Gods, was a carefully planned city once covering eight square miles. At its height, it is believed to have had a population of around 200,000 and was far more advanced than any European city of its time. For centuries, Teotihuacán was the Mesoamerican region's cultural, religious, political, economic, and social center. The massive temples of the Sun, the Moon, the

Citadel, and the various palaces, plazas, and paved streets are said to have been built by a pre-Aymara civilization. Once again, another incredible site, the builders of which are unidentified before one considers the Anunnaki paradigm.

According to archeologists, Teotihuacán was a vibrant metropolis and ceremonial center pre-dating the Aztecs civilization by several centuries. It must have been inhabited by thousands of people, but it is impossible to say who they were or where they came from. It is believed that its decline began suddenly around 650 AD and that by 740 AD it was completely abandoned. But no one knows why.

Though archaeologists have long been fascinated with the site, Teotihuacán's culture and history are still largely mysterious. The civilization left massive ruins, but no trace has yet been found of a writing system and very little is known for sure about its builders, who were followed first by the Toltecs and then by the Aztecs. The Aztecs did not live in the city, but gave the place and its major structures their current names. They considered it the "Place of the Gods" and believed it was the place where the world had been created.

It is known that ultimately the Aztecs were conquered by the Spanish. What is interesting about this fact is that many archaeologists and anthropologists agree that the Spanish were not necessarily better soldiers than the Aztecs, but that they physically resembled the Aztec's depictions of their god Quetzalcoatl.

Symbolized as a feathered serpent, Quetzalcoatl is also apparently an historical figure of some sort. He supposedly brought culture, mathematics, astronomy, masonry, architecture, agriculture, knowledge of herbal medicine, law, arts, metallurgy and the concept of the calendar to the Aztec people. But he is physically pictured as entirely different form the natives of this region. Rather, he is depicted as light-skinned, with a long nose and beard. The Aztecs believed that he had arrived by a boat from the east and, after imparting his wealth of knowledge, sailed away again with a promise to return one day.

Relevant to our discussion here, why would the Aztecs have created a god-like figure not out of their own image? And where did he come from? Clearly, they had acquired vast knowledge—enough to construct a remarkably advance civilization—from a creature who had come from far away. Further, he looked nothing like them, but was entirely other. When one considers facts like these, it is impossible not to at least consider the possibility of an alien helping hand all those centuries ago.

Turning back to the original inhabitants of Teotihuacán, though, and their remarkable achievements even before the Aztecs came into the picture, we must examine the incredible ruins they left behind.

It is here, at Teotihuacán, that we find even more remarkable pyramids, mirroring those found in Egypt as well as on Mars. There are also a number of palaces and temples adorned with incredible murals and stone carvings—all of which demonstrate a high degree of sophisticated artistry and craftsmanship.

But let's focus our attention on the remarkable pyramids, since they have such incredible, inexplicable parallels with Egypt and Cydonia. First, there is the Pyramid of the Sun, which is the largest in the Teotihuacán complex. It is the third largest pyramid on earth and it dominates the landscape of these Mesoamerican ruins.

As you can see, the pyramid is stepped rather than smooth-sided—more like the earliest Egyptian Pyramids rather than the later ones. It once stood 210 feet high and 650 feet square. There was a wooden temple perched upon the top of the pyramid, looking out over the vast city below.

It is very interesting to note some of the similarities between The Pyramid of the Sun and the Great Pyramid of Giza. Considering their vast geographical distance from one another, it is revealing to examine the relationship between the measurements of each one.

First of all, they are nearly equal in their base perimeter measurements. Also, the Pyramid of the Sun is just about exactly half the height of the Great Pyramid. It's also clear that the ratio of each of their heights to the perimeters of their bases are both based on the mathematical ratio *pi*. While the base perimeter of the Pyramid of the Sun is 4*pi* times its height, the Great pyramid of Giza's base perimeter is 2*pi* times its height. Obviously, whoever constructed these pyramids had a similar advanced knowledge of geometry and sophisticated mathematics. Each of these builders also applied their knowledge to constructing remarkable similar pyramids—located at a massive distance from one another. It is impossible not to suspect some common factor here, an architect perhaps linking these two radically different civilizations.

There is another remarkable feature of the all the pyramids at Teotihuacán. Many of them contain a very thick layer of mica, which is definitely not to be found in the area. The closest source location for mica is Brazil, in fact—which is more than 2,000 miles away! Mica is a very delicate substance—flakey in texture, almost powdery. Yet massive amounts of it are to be found in the pyramids here, and they could only have been brought in large quantities from this great distance, supposedly in an era pre-dating the use of wheeled vehicles. How could it have traveled so far?

It's also noteworthy that the mica was used as an inner layer of these pyramids—that is, it is not visible from the outside. Therefore, its application must have been practical rather than aesthetic. Today, we know to use mica as an insulating substance in electronic and electrical devices. Was it being used for the same purpose in these ancient pyramids? If so, how did these mysterious ancients have the knowledge of its insulating powers?

Another remarkable thing about Teotihuacán is the layout of the city. It turns out to be a grid, clearly, offset by about 15.5 degrees from the cardinal points. The main avenue, known as the Street of the Dead, runs from 15°.5 east of north to 15°.5 west of south. The Pyramid of the Sun is oriented north of due west by this exact same amount, making it so that this Pyramid faces directly into the point of the setting sun—on August 13th. Because of this last fact, we know that the layout of Teotihuacán being slightly off the cardinal points is not due to a "misalignment" or error in calculations. Clearly, it is laid out very deliberately.

The layout of the city suggests that it was done with an advanced knowledge of astronomy. The Pyramid of the Moon is located at one end of the Street of the Dead, and is aligned with the Pyramid of the Sun so carefully that it creates a sight line across the two, marking the meridian. This would have allowed the ancient people who built these structures to have fixed the times of noon and midnight with perfect precision.

There are many remarkable facts about this ancient city that indicate advanced mathematics and astronomy. It is difficult to imagine that many of the particulars of its construction were achieved with only observational, "naked-eye" astronomy, as it is supposed these people would have had. Is it possible, then, that they had more technology—more assistance—than we usually suppose? The precise design of the entire city and its pyramids certainly leads us to this conclusion.

Maccu Picchu

In the Cuzco region of Peru, we find another famous wonder of ancient design. Located 8,000 feet above sea level, Maccu Picchu was constructed out of massive stone blocks with such great precision that even a razor blade would not fit between them. Studies indicate it would be impossible for conventional means to lift the stones from quarries far down the mountains to such incredible heights. Also, the structures include a series of alignments that measure the precession of the equinoxes.

Maccu Picchu is an impressive, towering citadel of stone cut from a series of escarpments. It was designed to fit together completely without mortar—like the ruins of Puma Punk in Bolivia—in such a precise way that the stones fit together perfectly. The engineering that went into this boggles the mind, and seems to soar far and away above stone working techniques we would normally associate with ancient knowledge. Like many of the other ruins we have discussed so far, it is difficult to imagine how this advanced architecture was achieved.

This remarkable citadel consists of a number of elaborately constructed palaces, temples, dwelling-places and storehouses. Narrow paths and lanes connect all the buildings, plazas and ceremonial platforms of Maccu Picchu to one another. One section is even completely cordoned off by a series of carefully constructed walls and ditches—

perhaps even the remains of what was once a moat.

It's generally acknowledged Maccu Picchu was at least in part constructed as a highly sophisticated astronomical observatory. The Intihuatana stone—or "Hitching Post of the Sun"—is thus named because it was designed to "hitch" the sun at the two equinoxes. At midday on each equinox, the sun is located directly above the pillar so that it casts no shadow. Not only that, but the Intihuatana gives indications of other celestial periods as well, including the solstices.

Maccu Picchu was discovered in 1911 by a Yale University lecturer and explorer named Hiram Bingham. He literally stumbled across it on a hike and in so doing, stumbled into one of the 20th centuries greatest archaeological finds and what is now known as one of the Seven Wonders of the World.

Even though Maccu Picchu is clearly a wonder, and we've now had a century to analyze it, historians are still largely unsure about what purpose this ancient citadel served. That is because—just as in Nazca, Puma Punku, and other wondrous megalithic sites—there is no written evidence or record to describe the purpose or the architects of its construction.

One interesting recent discovery at Maccu Picchu is in the form of archaeological findings. They have dug up several bits of ceramic and pieces of head modeling which clearly suggest the presence of persons outside the Incan culture. Clearly, the Incans were not the only ones to have lived here. This presence of ceramics and head models produced by peoples from much further afield—including from Lake Titicaca in Bolivia —indicates a network of some kind, at least. It is likely that there was more connection between and among these ancient peoples than is usually perceived. Perhaps they shared a common source of knowledge?

Okinawa and Yonaguni, Japan

Off the coast of Japan—in yet another distinct corner of the globe—we find a series of enigmatic underwater wonders. Over the last few years, divers and archaeologists have discovered an incredible series of massive stone ziggurats located approximately 80 feet beneath the surface of the sea. Clearly artificial and terra formed, these structures mimic other sites above ground on the islands of Japan. The last time these structures would have been above sea level and habitable was at least 10,000 years ago, before the end of the last ice age caused them to slip beneath the water.

So far, eight anomalous underwater sites have been discovered. Specifically, there are two sites that seem to be most noteworthy. One is located near the city of Naha in Okinawa. In it, there is clearly an example of a wall, with a right-angled block now encrusted with coral. Not only that, there are a series of remarkable pyramids—calling to mind several of the other megalithic sites we have discussed.

The other site is just off the southernmost tip of Japan, near the island Yonaguni. What we find here are a series of stone terraces—strangely reminiscent of the platforms of Maccu Picchu so far away. There are also a number of right-angled block walls, as well as a series of stone circles encompassing hexagonal columns.
At the Yonaguni site, there are clearly examples of archways and 90-degree corners, indicating deliberate architecture and knowledge of mathematics and engineering.

Current theories suggest that the wall at Okinawa is a remnant of a castle whereas the Yonaguni site may have been more ceremonial in its purpose.

Were these structures man-made? Are they natural, the product of chance biological process? Or is it some combination of both nature and human effort? Lending weight to the theory of human effort is what appears to be an encircling road. Also, there appear to be post holes that would have supported wooden structures long dissolved by now, and what appear to be steps cut into the stone. These features clearly resemble other examples of architecture found nearby, on the land. The mysterious, sunken ruins at Okinawa and Yonaguni have the Japanese wondering if their homeland was once part of a lost continent known as Mu.

There has been much debate as to whether these massive structures are man-made, but the balance of evidence now seems to lean in that direction. At Yonaguni, there are five irregular stone layers that clearly form a terraced platform. It is almost farcical to believe that this structure came about through natural processes. Clearly, there is the presence of a deliberate hand here.

Professor Masaaki Kimura is a marine geologist at the University of the Ryukyus in Okinawa. After several years spent studying all eight of these puzzling sites, he is convinced that the monuments are man made. According to Kimura, they have been left by an unknown ancient civilization. He asserts that if the five terraced layers of the Yonaguni site had been the result of nature's carving work, there would be a significant amount of debris from the erosion collected around the area. To date, no rock fragments have been found. Therefore, this area must have been purposefully constructed, especially Yonaguni.

As with the other sites we've looked at, the construction of the Japanese sites clearly indicates a highly advanced understanding of geometry, architecture and engineering. They have not been positively dated, but the indications are that these ruins must be at least 10,000 years old, judging from the depth at which they have been buried beneath the water. Some suggest that they are even older, perhaps 12,000 years old. Yet, once again, there is no indication of who built them, or why, or—perhaps most importantly —how? Where did this knowledge of complex mathematics and architecture come from, all those years ago?

China

Up to four hundred massive earthen pyramids, solidified to rock hardness, are located within remote areas of China. Although the government does not allow many to come near them, photographs have surfaced revealing some of them to be as much as a mile on a side.

These pyramids were virtually unknown until recently. They are historic monuments that have stood the test of many years and weathered the elements with fortitude. The first hint of these pyramids was uncovered quite by accident towards the end of World War II by a United States pilot named James Gaussman. On his return flight after a mission to aid the Chinese, heading back to his base in India, Gaussman's engine failed and he found himself flying at a very low altitude over the Xi'an desert. He caught sight of what appeared to be a massive white pyramid. Stunned by what he saw, Gaussman used the opportunity to take photographs and filed a special report with the U.S. government later.

Another U.S. pilot, who had heard of Gaussman's "Great White" pyramid, flew close enough to it in 1947 to catch a glimpse. He estimated that it stood 1500 feet high— three times the height of the Great Pyramid of Giza! The Chinese authorities continued to keep this massive pyramid a secret, though, and managed to hide it from international investigation. German investigator Hartwig Hausdorf did somehow manage to gain access to the carefully patrolled airspace above Xi'an and attempted to capture photos of the mysterious Chinese pyramid himself, but he was unable to catch a glimpse. Nonetheless, he detailed his discoveries of other interesting structures in the area, and he published these in his 1994 book titled "The White Pyramid."

In 2000, China finally acknowledged the existence of about 400 pyramids in the Shanxi region north of the Xi'an desert. These ancient remains are all much smaller than the legendary "Great White" pyramid, and have generally been classified as burial mounds. It is true that many of these structures serve the purpose of tombs, but many suggest that they may have had a different, more mysterious purpose in antiquity. Even Hausdorf asserts the possibility that their origins may be extra-terrestrial.

The Chinese pyramid known as the Qin Shihuang Pyramid is another source of mystery. At this site, an impressive army of earthen figures can be found. It has come to be known as the "Terracotta Army," and is attributed to the Emperor Qin Shihuang. It is thought that the Emperor had these figures built as a representation of his army. Stretching nearly a mile in length, the figures depict soldiers and horses in exquisite detail —no two figures are the same.

The pyramid of Qin Shihuang is approximately 250 feet high now, but it once must have stood about 380 feet. The width of its base is approximately 1130 by 1150 feet. The pyramid has been carefully covered over with dirt and vegetation so that access to the main chamber is completely blocked. No one knows what may be found inside there when it is finally excavated. Perhaps there will be something within this pyramid to explain the mystery of these ancient marvels.

No one knows how old these Chinese pyramids are. It is possible to date many of them to particular dynasties, but not all. It is evident that many are far older. One ancient civilizations researcher and author, Graham Hancock, analyzed an aerial photograph of the group of pyramids located to the east of Xi'an. He found that the layout of these pyramids coincided perfectly with the constellation Gemini—but not as Gemini appears in the night sky today. Rather, as Gemini would have appeared on the spring equinox in 10,500 B.C.

At this point, you surely are drawing the parallel between this information and the arrangement of the Pyramids and Sphinx on the Giza plateau—also reflecting the appearance of a constellation in the night sky of antiquity. In the case of Egypt, the constellation is Orion, as it would have appeared in approximately 10,500 B.C. In China, the constellation is Gemini. Why would these pyramidal groupings so far from one another on the Earth's surface share such remarkable traits? And if this is so, then isn't it also logical that the pyramidal groupings in the Cydonia region of Mars are connected to these pyramids here on the Earth?

Cahokia

From Egypt to England, from Japan and China to South America, there is evidence of monumental ancient ruins all over the Earth. North America is no exception. Here, in the state of Illinois, we find an ancient North American site that includes massive mounds of earth of various sizes and shapes. Recently, one of these mounds at Cahokia was drilled into and this revealed a heretofore unknown

—and quite unexpected—solid rock core of what is thought to be limestone.

Located in the American Bottom floodplain between East Saint Louis and Collinsville in southwestern Illinois, this site covering over six square miles is the home of 120 earthen mounds that are clearly of human design and construction. No one knows who built these mounds or what was their purpose, but early European explorers first recorded their presence. According to these records, the mounds were shaped into distinct designs and suggest the evidence of a powerful ancient culture. One of the mounds was recorded by the early European explorers to have risen to 1,000 feet, making it the largest man-made mound in North America.

Other evidence was found as well—evidence that indicates the presence of a long-forgotten culture. Excavation efforts at Cahokia have uncovered enigmatic artifacts including stone pipes and tools made from copper and mica. There is also significant evidence of highly advanced engineering techniques and complex city planning within what was once a massive compound of cities and associated suburbs. According to these findings, researchers have concluded that whatever civilization existed at Cahokia all those centuries ago was massive. It must have had more than 15,000 residents at its height. Not only that, but a number of suburbs and agricultural centers branched out from around the city in every direction, suggesting a regional population of more than 40,000 people. If this was so, the Cahokian civilization must have been one of the world's largest ancient metropolitan areas.

It is not known what factors contributed to what must have been a massive population explosion in this area at some long-forgotten point in time. Evidence suggests that the region went from a population of 1,000 to 40,000 within a mere 100 years! How could this area have conquered so many challenges standing in the way of supporting so many people? Other regions dated around the same time are known to have struggled unsuccessfully against such challenging factors as food shortage, sanitation issues and unchecked disease. How could these mysterious Cahokians have supported themselves and overcome these very real challenges of the ancient world?

They must have had a brilliant level of city planning, technological knowledge and organization unrivalled by even the Ancient Romans. Clearly, there was a complex infrastructure of living centers as well as agricultural and production centers to support this ancient civilization. Yet no records exist which can possibly explain this.

What is perhaps even more mysterious is that at some point the civilization experienced a massive downfall. After what is estimated to have been about 250 years of thriving success, the entire civilization simply vanished. Theories as to why this happened so suddenly include the proposition of a changing climate, a miniature ice age, a great war, or some other inexplicable and sudden breakdown in civic structure. Yet, none of these theories is entirely borne out by the little evidence that remains.

It is interesting, in light of this, to take into consideration the legends that certain North American tribes passed down surrounding the disappearance of the Cahokians. According to these legends, there came a time when the thriving Cahokian civilization was at risk of being wiped out by rampant famine and disease. Teetering on the precipice of total obliteration, the Cahokians were suddenly visited by a number of robed beings—beings who came from the sky.

These extra-terrestrial visitors offered the Cahokians advanced knowledge and technology—essentially giving them the information they needed to save themselves from extinction. This advanced knowledge gave them the resources they needed not only to survive, but also to prosper and to become one of the world's most powerful civilizations. However, according to the ancient legend, the visitors "from the sky" told the Cahokians they would return in 500 years' time to collect payment from them.

The Cahokians agreed to this and, armed with advanced information and tools, they went on to become the most progressive civilization in the world. They all but forgot about the ones who had given them this gift. Then, according to the legend, the ground one day began to shake and fire rained down from the heavens. Hundreds of beings came, once again "from the sky," to claim their payment. The Cahokian civilization no longer wanted to pay their debt. Instead, they ran to the mounds they had created as a means of channeling their psychic energy and attempted to battle the beings from the sky. A great war ensued and the Cahokians ultimately lost to these far more advanced beings—the original source of their own remarkable knowledge.

What I have just related is a legend passed down to explain the disappearance of the Cahokian civilization. There is no more concrete evidence to support this legend than there is to support any of the theories of climate change or civil breakdown offered by mainstream science. It is important to note, however, that this legend has been around since before the indigenous people of this area could have possibly seen a person travel by airplane, or in fact come here from "the sky." Where do these images come from, then, is the question? Why are there so many legends and mythologies that include visitors who come from the sky?

Sacsahuaman

At the northern edge of Cuzco, Peru, we find a massive walled complex made of polished stones. As at Puma Punku, each of the massive boulders that makes up this complex is fitted together with baffling precision, and held in place without the aid of mortar. The stones fit so closely together that you could not slip a razor blade or even a blade of grass between them. The blocks also have precisely rounded corners and a wide spectrum of shapes that interlock.

In fact, the stones used to construct Sacsahuaman are the largest discovered in any of the prehispanic America constructions, and the way in which they are fitted together is unrivalled anywhere. The walls are generally about 18 feet tall and the longest of them is over 12,000 feet long. The volume of stone is estimated to be over 6,000 cubic meters, and the largest of the blocks is nearly 200 tons in weight. Again, it is a wonder how the people who built this place could have moved these rocks all the way up to the top of this mountain from the quarry so far away.

And it is even more of a mystery how they had the mathematics and technology to assemble walls like this. The andesite rock was supposedly cut in these elaborate ways by bronze or stone tools, but this is impossible. No one has yet been able to chip or cut andesite with any implement, much less bronze. There is nothing in the world that rivals the brilliance of how these walls were built. And the truth is, though this is assumed to be an Incan site, no-one really knows how long it has been here.

This series of immense terraced walls known as Sacsahuaman is situated high above the city of Cuzco, looking down upon the valley to the southeast. Because of its general shape and altitude, Sacsahuaman is presumed to have been a fortress of some kind. Analysis of pottery found at the site indicate that early occupants date back at least a millennium.

Sometime in the mid-1500's, a man named Carcilaso de la Vega wrote these words about

Sacsahuaman: "....this fortress surpasses the constructions known as the seven wonders of the world. For in the case of a long broad wall like that of Babylon, or the colossus of Rhodes, or the pyramids of Egypt, or the other monuments, one can see clearly how they were executed...how, by summoning an immense body of workers and accumulating more and more material day by day and year by year, they overcame all difficulties by employing human effort over a long period. But it is indeed beyond the power of imagination to understand now these Indians, unacquainted with devices, engines, and implements, could have cut, dressed, raised, and lowered great rocks, more like lumps of hills than building stones, and set them so exactly in their places. For this reason, and because the Indians were so familiar with demons, the work is attributed to enchantment."

Garcilaso de la Vega was born here, in approximately 1530, and he was raised here. He spend his life living next to this megalithic structure, and he had not the remotest idea of how it was built. There was no story passed on within his culture explaining this wonder. When he wrote this, nearly 500 years ago, the mystery of Sacsahuaman's construction was as remote and unattainable to him as it is to us today. When was this place built? And by whom? And where is their story? Perhaps this place is far, far older than we thought.

It is also most important to note the arrangement of the site at Sacsahuaman and its relationship to the city. The site consists of a large plaza big enough to hold thousands of people. It is clear that once there was a complex system of storage rooms in the complex as well, once containing military equipment, all contributing to the belief that it was used as some type of fortress. Another thing that excavations of the site have made clear is that there were once very tall towers and buildings with large windows overlooking the city. Archaeologists attest that the walls of Sacsahuaman once rose ten feet higher than the remnants that still stand there. The

Spanish conquistadors ransacked and used many of the materials to construct houses and cathedrals, hence much of the rock has been moved to other areas.

The most famous area of Sacsahuaman is that which contains the plaza and the three largest terraced walls. Many believe that the complex was deliberately constructed in such a way that, when viewed from above with the city of Cuzco in the picture, together forms the head of a puma.

As we move through our analysis of the Earth's megaliths, don't we seem to hear more and more echoes from one to the other? The deliberate formation of an image of a puma—a type of cat. A cat—like the Sphinx, which faced so long ago directly into the constellation of Leo, the Lion. To arrange the fortress of Sacsahuaman in this manner required an aerial viewpoint, as with all of those lines on the Nazca planes. How could a culture this ancient have had such an ability? Unless, as these echoes suggest, all of these places are connected by a common helper. A helper who shared advanced technologies and abilities with the ancient peoples so they could achieve these architectural miracles.

Ollantaytambo

Fifty kilometers from Maccu Picchu stands Ollytaytambo, a huge citadel that is believed to have been used as a fortress and a temple. The archaeological site and town of Ollantaytambo lie on the banks of the Patakancha River, with the main settlement on the left and a smaller compound known at Araqhama on the right. On a hilltop known as Cerro Bandalista, behind Araqhama, stands the primary ceremonial center presumed to have been built by the Incans. Located at an altitude of some 9,000 feet above sea level to the north of the Sacred Valley, this site remained unfinished. It is not known why construction was stopped on this massive project.

Here, too, the stone technology applied to the building of this site is both highly advanced and difficult to explain. The remarkable Sun Temple is made out of a pink granite known as red porphyry, and it consists of a number of massive boulders.

The quarry from which these boulders came is called Kachiqhata or Salt Slope. It is nearly three miles away from the location of the Sun Temple, all the way across the valley near the south-western mountains. The boulders must have been at least partially carved in the quarry, then somehow transported to the bottom of the valley. It is difficult to imagine the process that could have moved these huge boulders the necessary three miles, but it is certain that an elaborate series of levers and pulleys must have been used, not to mention a huge amount of manpower. Some stones, referred to as "tired stones," never made the journey and remain to this day abandoned along the route from quarry to citadel.

Even more remarkable is the way in which these boulders have been fitted together. The huge, irregularly shaped, many-sided blocks have been so precisely connected in a series of interlocking patterns that the whole structure is able to withstand Earthquakes. A remarkable achievement for an ancient culture, and one that nobody can fully explain. As with Puma Punku, Maccu Piccu and many others, it would have been impossible to build this megalith without advanced knowledge of stonemasonry and geometry.

All the main quarries of Ollyantaytambo are in a ravine across the Urubamba River nearly three miles from the town. It is clear that in the three quarries known as Mullup'urku, Kantirayoq and Sirkusirkuyoq there is a great deal of the red porhyry out of which this site is built. It is certain the materials came from here. Yet, how were they carried so far? How were they so precisely cut and fit into such elaborate interlocking patterns, rendering these structures nearly invulnerable to Earthquakes? What tools did they have that would cut this rock? This is not an easy task now, with all the tools and knowledge of the modern age. How was it done so well here… so long ago?

Earth's First Civilization – Sumer

My research led me back almost 6,000 years ago in our history to the oldest civilization we have on record. At that time, we would have found this civilization established in a fertile strip of land between the Tigris and Euphrates valley known as Sumer. Almost overnight, from right out of the Stone Age, "Sumerian Civilization" emerged into the land that is now southern Iraq. It has been called Mesopotamia and it has been called Babylon —but the first culture located here were the Sumerians.

What is amazing about the Sumerian culture is that over 100 of the firsts needed for an advanced civilization can be attributed to them. In this section, I will talk about some of the remarkable discoveries, inventions and processes of the Sumerians—many of which we still use today.

As we look at these remarkable contributions by the ancient Sumerian culture, keep in mind that this is a civilization nearly 6,000 years old. So far, we have examined some of the amazing technical skills and advanced knowledge of several ancient cultures responsible for the mysterious megalithic structures across the globe. We will see many of the same remarkable developments as we look at the Sumerian culture, and the question we must continually ask ourselves is: did they do it alone?

Agriculture:

The Sumerians grew barley, chickpeas, lentils, millet, wheat, turnips, dates, onions, garlic, lettuce, leeks and mustard. They also raised cattle, sheep, goats, and pigs. They used oxen as their primary beasts of burden and donkeys as their primary transport animal. Sumerians hunted fish and fowl.

Sumerian agriculture depended heavily on irrigation. The irrigation was accomplished by the use of canals, channels, dykes, weirs and reservoirs. The canals required frequent repair and continual removal of silt. The government required individuals to work on the canals, although the rich were able to exempt themselves.

Using the canals, farmers would flood their fields and then drain the water. Next they let oxen stomp the ground and kill weeds. They then dragged the fields with pickaxes. After drying, they plowed, harrowed, raked thrice, and pulverized with a mattock.

Sumerians harvested during the dry fall season in three-person teams consisting of a reaper, a binder, and a sheaf arranger. The farmers would use threshing wagons to separate the cereal heads from the stalks and then use threshing sleds to disengage the grain.

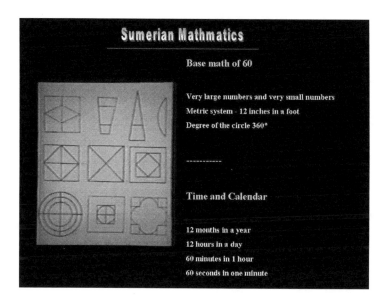

Sumerian Mathmatics

Base math of 60

Very large numbers and very small numbers
Metric system - 12 inches in a foot
Degree of the circle 360*

Time and Calendar

12 months in a year
12 hours in a day
60 minutes in 1 hour
60 seconds in one minute

Math:

Sumerian mathematics refers to any mathematics of the people of Mesopotamia, from the days of the early Sumerians to the fall of Babylon in 539 BC. Sumerian mathematical texts are plentiful and well edited. In respect of time they fall in two distinct groups: one from the Old Sumerian period (1830-1531 BC), the other mainly Seleucid from the last three or four centuries BC. In respect of content there is scarcely any difference between the two groups of texts.

123

Thus Sumerian mathematics remained constant, in character and content, for nearly two millennia. In contrast to the scarcity of sources in Egyptian mathematics, our knowledge of Sumerian mathematics is derived from some 400 clay tablets unEarthed since the 1850s. Written in Cuneiform script, tablets were inscribed while the clay was moist, and baked hard in an oven or by the heat of the sun. The majority of recovered clay tablets date from 1800 to 1600 BC, and cover topics which include fractions, algebra, quadratic and cubic equations and the Pythagorean theorem. The Sumerian tablet YBC 7289 gives an approximation accurate to five decimal places.

The Sumerian system of mathematics was sexagesimal (base-60) numeral system. From this we derive the modern day usage of 60 seconds in a minute, 60 minutes in an hour, and 360 (60×6) degrees in a circle. The Sumerians were able to make great advances in mathematics for two reasons. Firstly, the number 60 is a Highly composite number, having divisors 1, 2, 3, 4, 5, 6, 10, 12, 15, 20, 30 and 60, facilitating calculations with fractions. Additionally, unlike the Egyptians and Romans, the Sumerians and Indians had a true place-value system, where digits written in the left column represented larger values (much as in our base ten system: $734 = 7 \times 100 + 3 \times 10 + 4 \times 1$).

The Sumerians made extensive use of pre-calculated tables to assist with arithmetic. For example, two tablets found at Senkerah on the Euphrates in 1854, dating from 2000 BC, give lists of the squares of numbers up to 59 and the cubes of numbers up to 32. The Sumerians used the lists of squares together with the formulas to simplify multiplication.

The Sumerians did not have an algorithm for long division. Instead they based their method on a table of reciprocals. Numbers whose only prime factors are 2, 3 or 5 (known as 5-smooth or regular numbers) have finite reciprocals in sexagesimal notation, and tables with extensive lists of these reciprocals have been found.

As well as arithmetical calculations, Sumerian mathematicians also developed algebraic methods of solving equations. Once again, these were based on pre-calculated tables.

The Sumerians knowledge of mathematics—in fact they practically invented the mathematics we use today!—cannot help but strike us as remarkable. For a culture thriving 6,000 years ago, they clearly had some incredible resources of information. While I by no means intend to dismiss the marvelous fact of human ingenuity at any point in my discussions here, it is important to consider that perhaps the Sumerians had access to more knowledge than we realize. As I will discuss in depth later in the book, we have every reason to believe that the Anunnaki were integral to this fact. Where did the Anunnaki come from? They came from the sky.

Schools:

Schools were attached to the main temple in the town and were referred to as the edubba. The head teacher maintained the title of school father or unmia. Each school father had assistants that were known as big brothers. It was the job of the school father to maintain focus, discipline, and provide most of the instruction. Big brothers would provide assistance to pupils, prepare clay tablets for writing, and at times also discipline the students. Students were continually reprimanded for mistakes. Humiliation and negative comments were commonplace. Students could also be hit with a stick.

Eventually, subjects other than scribing were added to the daily curriculum in schools. Students learned about mathematics, law, biology, astronomy, economics, agriculture and the Sumerian language. Creative writing only took place in schools. In Sumer, only upper class males went to school; girls were not allowed to attend. Males would go to school for approximately twenty-five days a month and be in session year-round, from sunrise to sunset. Most males went to school to study to become scribes. Scribes recorded all business transactions, legal matters, and stories in ancient form of writing called cuneiform. Being a scribe was a very prestigious and high-paying job in the Sumerian cities.

Students would spend their mornings copying myths and epics. Their afternoons focused on critiquing and refining their writing. The usage of numerous clay tablets and the constant copying of written material lead to the naming of Sumerian schools as "Tablet Houses."

As we can see, the Sumerian culture place a high value on education and on effective systems. Typically, this type of development is associated with advance levels of civilization. Let us not forget that the Sumerians developed much of what we still view as essential to a civilization—thousands of years in the past, before the Dark Ages. We are about to look at their legal system in the next section, which was also fairly complex.

Courts:

Although we don't know much about Sumerian law, scholars agree that the Code of Hammurabi, written by a Babylonian monarch, reproduces Sumerian law fairly exactly. Sumerian law, as represented in Hammurabi's code, was a law of exact revenge. This is revenge in kind: "an eye for an eye, a tooth for a tooth, a life for a life," and reveals to us that human law has as its fundamental basis revenge. Sumerian law was also only partly administered by the state; the victim had to bring the criminal to court. Once there, the court mediated the dispute, rendered a decision, and most of the time a court official would execute the sentence, but often it fell on the victim or the victim's family to enforce the sentence. Finally, Sumerian law recognized class distinctions; under Sumerian law, everyone was not equal under the law.

Harming a priest or noble person was a far more serious crime than harming a slave or poor person; yet, the penalties assessed for a noble person who commits a crime were often far harsher than the penalties assessed for someone from the lower classes that committed the same crime.

Code of Hammurabi

Hammurabi's Law Code was the earliest known law code in existence. King Hammurabi is remembered for his 'Code' or collection of laws. It was modeled on existing laws, but this was the largest law code assembled. The Code has 282 provisions which dealt with many aspects of life, including family rights, trade, slavery, tariffs, taxes, prices and wages. The Code tells us much about Babylonian society. The Code of Hammurabi is inscribed on a stone slab over 2 meters (6ft) high. At the top, the King is shown receiving laws from the Babylonian sun god, Shamash.

The laws are not the same for rich and poor, but the weak were given some protection against the tyranny of the strong. The Code was not the only law code in Mesopotamia, but the only one written in stone. The code was based on retribution, not justice, and varied unfairly between social classes.

Though in some ways the Code of Hammurabi strikes our modern eyes as a bit violent and primitive, it noteworthy that the Sumerians developed a legal system that was so specific. Not only that, we can see some of the foundations of our own modern legal ideas underpinning the Code as we read through it.

THE CODE

1. If any one ensnare another, putting a ban upon him, but he can not prove it, then he that ensnared him shall be put to death.

2. If any one bring an accusation against a man, and the accused go to the river and leap into the river, if he sink in the river his accuser shall take possession of his house. But if the river prove that the accused is not guilty, and he escape unhurt, then he who had brought the accusation shall be put to death, while he who leaped into the river shall take possession of the house that had belonged to his accuser.

3. If any one bring an accusation of any crime before the elders, and does not prove what he has charged, he shall, if it be a capital offense charged, be put to death.

4. If he satisfy the elders to impose a fine of grain or money, he shall receive the fine that the action produces.

5. If a judge try a case, reach a decision, and present his judgment in writing; if later error shall appear in his decision, and it be through his own fault, then he shall pay twelve times the fine set by him in the case, and he shall be publicly removed from the judge's bench,

and never again shall he sit there to render judgment.

Marriage:

In western society some aspects of modern family relationships and composition can be traced to ancient Mesopotamia and Babylonia. Ideas such as the wedding, marriage and divorce began developing then. Through innumerable legal documents from the Sumerian to the Seleucid period, we see the individual as father, son, brother or husband. The root of these relationships started with a proposal, followed by the marriage contract, and ending with the wedding. The young Mesopotamian couple then chose where to live. In certain circumstances, the male had to decide whether to have another wife or a concubine. In no time, the newlyweds begot children. The father, as the head of the family, had complete authority over them. This authority extended to such matters as adoption and inheritance. How big the family unit got depended on where in Mesopotamia it formed.

The family unit in Mesopotamia was small and restricted for the most part. In certain regions of southern Babylonia, however, clan-like or even tribal organizations of some sort existed. In neo-Babylonian times, a measure of family consciousness appeared in the form of ancestral family names for identification purposes. The first step in creating a family unit, whether small or clan-like, is of course the marriage. Ironically, for most of history, it left the prospective bride out of the decision-making process.

Marriage was regarded as a legal contract, and divorce as its breakup were similarly affected by official procedures. The future husband and his father-in-law agreed on a contract and if a divorce occurred, the father-in-law was entitled to satisfaction. The contract made between the suitor and the father of the expected bride stipulated a price for the maiden's hand. She received the sum given to the father. If the marriage did not produce children then the price the groom had paid for his wife was returned to him upon on her death, if it had not been returned previously. Lack of children was not the only reason for returning the price paid for the wife; her death could create a refund.

Once married, the girl became a full member of her future husband's family. If he died, she would marry one of his brothers or, if he lacked brothers, one of his near relatives. If these conditions did not take place, her father returned all his rights over her, and gave back all the presents that she had received except those consumed. Conversely, if the girl died, and her intended husband did not want to marry one of her sisters, he would take back all the presents that he had given her. An agreement once reached indicated that the actual wedding ceremony could now take place.

I enjoy this proverb also found amongst Sumerian writing...."Man for his pleasure, Marriage. On thinking it over....Divorce."

Beer:

The oldest proven records of brewing are about 6,000 years old and refer to the Sumerians. It is said that the Sumerians discovered the fermentation process by chance. A seal around 4,000 years old is a Sumerian "Hymn to Ninkasi," the goddess of brewing. This "hymn" is also a recipe for making beer. No one knows today exactly how this occurred, but it could be that a piece of bread or grain became wet and a short time later, it began to ferment and a inebriating pulp resulted. These early accounts, with pictograms of what is recognizably barley, show bread being baked then crumbled into water to make a mash, which is then made into a drink that is recorded as having made people feel "exhilarated, wonderful and blissful!" It could be that baked bread was a convenient method of storing and transporting a resource for making beer. The Sumerians were able to repeat this process and are the first civilized culture to brew beer. They had discovered a "divine drink" which certainly was a gift from the gods.

Astronomy:

The Sumerians recorded the movements of the planets over hundreds of years. A Sumerian priest who could read the cuneiform text about astronomy could tell you 50 years in advance on what day there would be a lunar eclipse. They had very accurate astronomical information, which we have confirmed with our modern science. They actually listed the distance between the outer planets and correctly cited the color of the outer planets such as Uranus and Neptune. When we sent the Galileo and Voyager probes into deep space in the late 70's and early 80's they took the first color pictures on the outer planets. NASA's pictures exactly matched the Sumerian descriptions from 6,000 years ago as bluish-green planets.

Evidence of their knowledge can be seen is this amazing cylinder seal found in the British museum. Where as a backdrop to the drawing, we see our solar system with all the planets we know of and the sun listed correctly in the center. We did not know the sun was in the center of our solar system well into the time of Copernicus and Galileo. They used advanced mathematics combined with new advances in the telescope to make these conclusions. But somehow the Sumerian culture from 6,000 years ago already knew this information. But how did they know?

The Sumerians were the first ones to divide
the heavens into 12 parts, assigning each
section of the sky with a symbol. Remember
the number 12 as we will see it has a key
influence in our our modern culture directly
passed down from the Sumerian culture. As
we move into later sections of the book, we
will discuss in more depth the profound
importance of the 12 signs of the zodiac and
the precession of the equinox as seen in the
constellations of the night sky.

Bear in mind that the Sumerians identified the
12 constellations of the zodiac and the
precession of the equinox—and we still use

the same system today. They clearly had a remarkable system for understanding the night sky, and they were quite familiar with a race of beings who came to them from out of that sky. In fact, with any study of ancient Sumerian texts, it becomes more and more clear that the Sumerians did not come up with everything they knew just on their own. As we move on, keep in mind also the image of the astronaut so clearly carved into the Nazca plain that we discussed earlier. Keep in mind the inexplicable faces of the megalithic statues on Easter Island, the remarkable astronomical significance of the arrangement of the Egyptian Pyramids and the massive stones that make up Stonehenge. You must ask yourself—what is the connection among all these things?

Writing:

Probably the most significant contribution the Sumerians made to human history and culture is the written word. The Sumerian form of writing was called cuneiform script. It consisted of someone using what looked like an over sized screw driver that they would then turn and twist into wet clay, leaving the symbols behind. Cuneiform script has over 400 characters. That is pretty amazing for the first alphabet we have on record.

What is more amazing is what they wrote in the clay. They wrote most of their text in wet clay, then would place these clay tablets into a stove and make them into stone. They literally coined the phrase "writing in stone."

Along with their stone tablet texts were small round stone cylinder seals that had reversed carved images cut into the stone. And when pressed into wet clay they leave the positive imprinted image. It was quite an ingenious way to have an ancient printing press. They could easily create tablets and images to spread throughout the culture.

They used this system of writing to record all kinds of information. Mainly it was used to record daily transactions of sales, or texts for education.

Medical Science:

Of all the contributions of the Sumerian culture, some of the most stunning information is certainly to be found in the field of medical science. It is clear that this 6,000 year old civilization had highly sophisticated knowledge of fertility and genetic science. For an ancient civilization to be doing this type of experimentation is certainly surprising. We must ask ourselves what were they up to? We will see, as we look at this in more detail, the the mysterious race of living gods known as the Anunnaki had everything to do with this.

Recent advances in DNA research have established that there was an Eve who lived about 250 to 270 thousand years ago, a first mother from who all modern humans stem, no matter what their racial heritage. [In 1987, scientists from the Universities of California and Michigan announced that all human beings descended from a single mitochondrial Eve: who lived in Africa.]

A few years after this discovery, it came to light that there was also an actual Adam. Finally, genetic advances made test-tube babies possible by mixing the male sperm with the female egg and re-implanting it.

What is even more remarkable about this is that it corroborates what the Sumerians already knew *6,000 years ago*. We have recovered some of the records related to the Anunnaki—in Sumerian, as I have mentioned previously, this means "those who from heaven to Earth came." And in these ancient records are descriptions of highly advance genetic engineering, things it is very difficult to imagine a culture knowing about 6,000 years ago.

Interestingly, these records describe a laboratory where the genetic experiments took place. It turns out it was located in east central Africa—exactly where the mitochondrial DNA of the original "Eve" I mentioned earlier was discovered. It is also noteworthy that, as a species, we have gone from our original inception to possessing the capacity for space travel within only 250,000 years. This is a relatively rapid time period, and it does not correspond to the millions of years it took for previous species such as Homo Erectus to evolve. We are, ourselves, an anomoly, developmentally speaking.

So what is all this saying? You wonder how is it possible, how could they know? How, as another example, could the Sumerian symbol of the entwined serpents, that we still use today to denote medicine and healing and biology, be 6,000 years ago, the symbol of Enki, who engaged in genetic engineering to bring about the Adam? It was then as now a symbol for DNA. It represents the famous double helix of DNA.

Notice in this image, on the top, the two entwined snakes and the ladder like ribbons between the serpents bodies.....does it remind you of anything?

Remember that these images are thousands of years old. Today we still use the image of the entwined serpent as a sign of medicine. This carried over from ancient times. What does the emblem of entwined serpents, the symbol for medicine and healing to this very day, represent?

The discovery by modern science of the double helix structure of DNA offers the answer: The entwined serpents emulated the structure of the genetic code, the secret knowledge of which enabled the creation of the Adam. The first man the Anunnaki created called the "Adam."

If the Sumerians were conducting genetic experiments and had the capacity to create human life with test tubes several thousand years ago—where did they get their knowledge? Perhaps more importantly, why were they developing their knowledge of genetic engineering? What was the purpose of such experimentation? In the next section, we will dive into these questions much more deeply. Clearly, the Anunnaki hold the key.

The Anunnaki - Those Who From Heaven to Earth Came

In the early 1900's British archeologists started doing excavations in the ancient Sumerian city of UR. Many of the artifacts and tablets spoke of beings called the Anunnaki and depicted these beings with wings. Why did ancient man depict the Anunnkai with wings? This seems very similar to angels in the modern bible. The answer is quite simple if we look at more modern references. In ancient times, man did not understand technology. So anything flying in the skies of

Earth had to be alive. Depicting the Anunnkai with wings leads me to believe the Sumerians were trying to say that the Anunnaki had the power of flight. Since ancient man did not understand technology, they gave the Anunnaki wings to symbolically represent their power of flight.

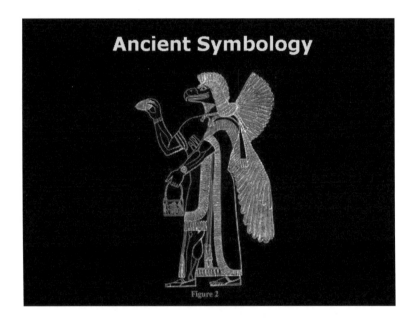

Figure 2

We find references to this same phenomenon in other ancient cultural records as I have discussed elsewhere in the book—beings who were clearly others, who had arrived from the sky. And we must not forget the astronaut and the other images constructed upon the Nazca plain—images that could only have come if the designer had an aerial viewpoint.

If you look at modern references to when we landed the first Apollo mission on the moon, the words used to mark that event were" Houston, the Eagle has landed." Even the Apollo symbol was an eagle. Does this mean 6,000 years from now people will wonder why we were landing birds on the moon?

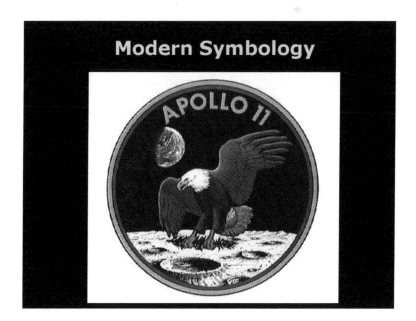

As archeologists over the years have gone over the cuneiform tablets left by the Sumerians, they have found countless references to these Anunnaki—which in Sumerian means literally "those who from heaven to Earth came." In these writings, they were described as beings who came from the sky, who had the power of flight, who taught them things, who gave them resources and information. As you might imagine, most of the tablets describing the Anunnaki were thrown into a big MYTH pile and basically left untouched to this day. What is truly stunning is how the Sumerian stories relating to the Anunnaki are similar to so many other "myths" we find in the study of other ancient cultures.

Finally, with regard to the Sumerian cuneiform tablets, something remarkable happened. The assistant curators of the museum found a set of tablets and began to decipher a very familiar story. On this ancient stone tablet was recorded a story about how a Sumerian man is chosen by god to build a great ship. He is instructed to take his family and animals and even plants onto the boat because there is going to be a great flood—and he must preserve their lives on his boat while everything on land is swept away. Sound familiar? This tablet was thousands of years older than any other biblical source of information. Clearly, they had found the original source for "Noah's Ark." A little bit later, I will discuss in more detail the true significance of the story of Noah's Ark.

The curator ran out of the room with his hands in the air shouting, "I can't believe it, I can't believe it!"

The Epic of Gilgamesh is widely known today. The first modern translation of the epic was published in the early 1870s by George Smith who found the tablet. More recent translations into English include one undertaken with the assistance of the American novelist John Gardner, and John Maier, published in 1984. In 2001, Benjamin Foster produced a reading in the Norton Critical Edition Series that fills in many of the blanks of the standard edition with previous material.

Scholars found many tablets that seem to parallel stories found in our modern biblical texts. But since Sumer is the oldest recorded civilization, did we find the original source of biblical information?

What really makes the Sumerian versions of these seemingly biblical stories different is the remarkable fact that they so often speak of these Anunnaki. It is clear that the Anunnaki are not another people like themselves—no, instead they are living gods to the Sumerians. They speak about how they came from heaven and live among them. Even though they live among them, there is still a sense of worship and an understanding that these Anunnaki are advanced.

The Sumerians left behind much more evidence of the Anunnaki than just the cuneiform tablets. They also took the trouble to produce a number of wall carvings depicting their interaction with these beings. They always drew the Anunnaki with wings on their backs, or coming down from heaven on a winged disk.

Of course, when British archeologists in the early 1900's were uncovering all this information, they considered it mythology. But why is it that so many of the images and stories left behind by other ancient cultures across the globe share so many similar echoes?

All the tablets that talked about the distance of the planets or what the outer planets looked like in space did not make any sense at the time. We did not discover Pluto until 1930. So many of these tablets talking about their GODS or events taking places in the "Heavens" were thought of as myths, and put into a big pile and ignored for the most part by academia.

Sumerian God coming to Earth

In the British museum alone, there are thousands of Sumerian tablets and only about one per cent of them have been translated up to this point. The tablets that haven been translated show that Sumerian knowledge was vast in many areas which modern science now confirms.

The area modern science has not yet been able to confirm is the stories they recorded about interaction with their living gods, the Anunnaki. The term Anunnaki simply means those who from heaven to Earth came. If you were to ask a Sumerian man, "How do you know all that you know?" he would respond "All we know, we were taught by the Anunnaki."

Remarkably, the depictions of the Anunnaki left by the Sumerians show us that we look very much like them. According to the Atrahasis tablets—a series of 7 tablets recording the Sumerian's creation stories—the Anunnaki told the Sumerian priests "we made you in our image and our likeness." Now, this has obvious biblical echoes, clearly. We are all familiar with the Christian idea that God created all of humanity in his image. But I'd like you to consider an even more literal interpretation of this statement—and hold it in your mind as we move into the next section of the book.

First, let's focus a bit more on the Atrahasis tablets. According to these 7 tablets, the

Anunnaki had come to Earth over 350,000 years ago and had a major influence on how our Earth as we know it came to be. The Anunnaki explained that they originally came to Earth seeking gold and other precious elements. On their own rise to a technological civilization, the Anunnaki had damaged their planet's atmosphere to a dangerous degree. They discovered, however, that using fine particulates of gold, they could shoot this into the atmosphere to help patch the holes in the planet's ozone. We know gold has several key properties in how we use it today. We line all the astronauts' spacesuit visors with gold, as it is an excellent reflector of heat.

The Anunnaki found large veins of gold deposited in southern Africa. They dispatched a team of 50 Anunnaki to the surface of Earth and began mining the gold out of the ground. They soon discovered the mining process was long and arduous. One of the leaders of the Anunnaki named Enkil suggested they create a worker race to mine the gold. He suggested using the primitive "ape man" that was evolving here on Earth as the slave race. But Enkil did not simply want to leave this ape man as he was. He wanted to place the Anunnaki's genetic marker on him. To do this, he would use genetic manipulation to combine 20% of the primitive genes with 80% of the more advanced Anunnaki genes. Thus, he would create a new being that would be "in their image and after their likeness."

There were several images that accompanied the texts explaining this creation process. The texts explain how one of the chief scientists, Ninharsad, tried several different attempts to create a working model. In his first version, the arm did not function. In the second model, the kidneys were not working. Until finally she created a perfect model, they called Lu-Lu Amelu. There were pictograms that accompanied this text showing Ninharsad holding up the first working model, the one they called 'the adam.'

It is important to note that this word, adam, appeared here in the Sumerian texts long before the bible. Interestingly, we later find it as the Hebrew word adamu—which means worker. Adam and Eve? Not just the product of biblical tales. It is now known that these "workers" really existed long before the bible was written. They were created by the Anunnaki.

Once the Anunnaki had the working Lu Lu Amelu, they soon decided that they wanted to have a much larger work force and decided to then upgrade the Lu Lu Amelu to have male and female. By copying their own genetic code onto the primitive man, they created a new version of Lu Lu Amelu that was now male and female, just like the Anunnaki.

At this point, the male and female could not actually procreate, because they were genetic hybrids. Yet, the Anunnaki needed more workers, so they practiced more and more genetic manipulation to make it possible for us to reproduce. Once this happened, we became quite numerous—became fruitful, if you will, and multiplied. Eventually, the species began moving out of the city centers and spreading out across the entire planet. At this point, think of all the megalithic structures across the planet and how we have discussed so many significant echoes from one to the other.

Ultimately, the Anunnaki began to procreate with their hybrid race (us) and children were born. This was considered taboo by their High Council and it created a big problem. How did the Anunnaki resolve this problem?

They created a flood. Because they could predict the flood by knowing when Nibiru—the tenth planet or Planet x which we will dicuss in more detail later—was scheduled to come back through the inner solar system again. This home planet of the Anunnaki came through the inner solar system on a periodic 3600 return—12,500 years ago, creating the flood that would wipe out the humans and genetic hybrids. Because Enki had created us, though, he was sympathetic and managed to save many human lives. Enki was the god, essentially, who told Noah to build an Ark. Or so we might say.

For years, we worked as their slaves. Evidence of what they taught us about construction, technology, science and mathematics is clearly found all over the Earth—from Mesopotamia to India to South America. There is nowhere on this plante the Anunnaki have not influenced.

Then, about 6,000 years ago, they decided to bring us to our independence. That explains the surprising, sudden appearance of the highly advanced civilization of Sumer. They began to let us go as slaves, and the Sumerians began to name human kings, forerunners of the population that would answer to the Anunnaki as gods. Many believe that some humans were deliberately genetically enhanced by their genes to create a ruling bloodline.

The humans chosen by their ancient alien gods were then taught technology, mathematics, advanced construction techniques, arts, crafts and all the other trappings of a great civilization.

The Sumerian creation tales not only tell about the creation of man, but also the creation of Earth. In the bible we have a consolidated version that says God created the heavens and Earth in 7 days. Well the Sumerian "7 tablets of creation" tell a much more detailed story about the creation of Earth.

The creation tablets state that our solar system was just starting to form and the planets had not become solid yet. An intruder planet appeared and fell under gravitational influence by the outer planets. It passed by Pluto, Uranus and Neptune. The intruder planet began to travel towards the inner part of our solar system. Our primitive planet Earth was labeled by the Sumerians as Tiamat. They explain that as the intruder planet passed through the inner part of the solar system, one of the large moons of this intruder planet collided into our primitive Earth (Tiamat). The collision cracked Tiamat in half, spewing out debris into the pattern we now see today as the asteroid belt. The bible calls this the hammered-out bracelet.

After the collision, Tiamat was thrust into a new orbit and the waters of Nibiru intermingled with the waters of Earth and life began to arise already whole and complete. A term for this is panspermia.

The Sumerian creation tales explain some very key aspects to our modern understanding of cosmology, and possibly how life on Earth began. For life to have naturally evolved here are Earth would have taken billions of years longer than the recorded history of Earth. The biological process of a living creature to take in nutrients and expel waste is extremely complex genetics. The idea that somehow life evolved on Earth from primordial soup and a bolt of lighting is just not accepted anymore. That is equivalent to a tornado ripping through a junkyard and somehow magically assembling a 747, the odds are too great for that to be the answer.

Panspermia is the hypothesis that "seeds" of life exist already all over the Universe, that life on Earth may have originated through these "seeds," and that they may deliver or have delivered life to other habitable bodies.

The related but distinct idea of exogenesis is a more limited hypothesis that proposes life on Earth was transferred from elsewhere in the Universe but makes no prediction about how widespread it is. Because the term "exogenesis" is more well-known, it tends to be used in reference to what should strictly speaking be called panspermia.

The Sumerian creation tales explain how the waters of Nibriu mingled with our Earth. Could this be the answer to how life arrived on Earth whole and complete? Nibiru being a much older planet, probably has had billions of years longer time for life to evolve. Or life to have arrived on Nibiru and then evolved much longer than life here on Earth.

The creation tale goes on to explain that the planet Nibiru becomes a permanent member of our solar system on a highly elliptical orbit. The Sumerians recorded this orbit to be 3,600 years to complete and they called this a shar. A solar year for Earth is 356 days to orbit the sun. Nibiru's orbit around the sun takes 3,600 years to complete one orbit.

If the Anunnaki come from Nibiru as the Sumerian have stated in their creation tales they would have a much longer life span compared to here on Earth. As an example, let's say someone from Earth travels to Nibiru and stays on that planet for one year. When they return to Earth, 3,600 years will have passed on Earth. But the person returning to Earth, has only aged 1 year. This point speaks to many of the biblical references with regards to ascending to heaven to enjoy a longer lifespan. Imagine if Jesus Christ was an Anunnaki and came here to Earth and established his following. Then he leaves Earth and returns to Nibiru for 1 year. When he returns back to Earth, he has only aged 1 year, but it has been 3,600 years on Earth.

If Nibiru does exist, our modern science might be able to see it. There are actual Sumerian tablets that show a man looking up while plowing a field. He is looking up to the sky with his hands shielding his eyes. In the sky you see circle emanating rays of light (the sun) and a cross emanating rays of light (Nibiru). The Sumerians were aware of a time when they could actually see Nibiru as it came close to the inner part of our solar system.

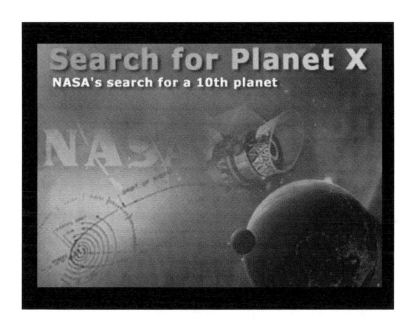

Search for Planet X
NASA's search for a 10th planet

The Search for Planet X

How might we see evidence for this planet being in our solar system? In the early 1990's, Dr. Robert Harrington—the lead astronomer for the Naval Observatory in Washington—suggested including another large planet in our solar system model. He could then explain many of the anomalies we currently see, such as why Uranus is tilted on its side. Or how Pluto and Neptune are possibly dislodged moons of Saturn. Dr. Harrington plotted an orbit of a planet with a very elliptical orbit coming out of the southern hemisphere towards the inner part of the solar system. His model very closely matched the description by the Sumerians of Nibiru being 4-8 times the size of Earth and depicted as having a very elongated orbit. Dr. Harrington also noted that based upon orbital perturbations in the outer planets, there should be another large planet out there. This simply means that all the planets are being pulled in one direction by some force that would suggest there should be some large body as the cause.

In more recent times, the search for a planet x can now be placed under a larger astronomical interest in looking for extra-solar planets. (Planets that are not a part of our solar system). In this process we have also created many new classifications about stars and planets we are imaging deep in space.

Another fascinating and recent astronomical discovery is that almost all the external solar systems we have imaged with Hubble appear to be binary, having 2 suns. So it stands to reason our solar system is probably binary as well, having 2 suns. But our second sun is a brown dwarf, a failed sun. This second sun might also have planets and debris that orbit around it. You will want to remember this piece of information as you read the final section of this book.

One theory proposed was by Dr. Richard Muller at Berkley University. He suggested a large planet called Nemesis may orbit our second sun. There is a large asteroid belt also near our second sun, which this planet passes through. Dr. Muller suggested this Nemesis planet would periodically over millions of years dislodge comets and debris from the outer asteroid belt called the Ourt cloud. This debris would be hurled to the inner part of our solar system, and this is what Dr. Muller suggested caused the extinction of the dinosaurs.

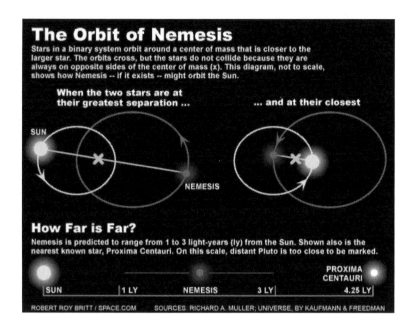

The Orbit of Nemesis

Stars in a binary system orbit around a center of mass that is closer to the larger star. The orbits cross, but the stars do not collide because they are always on opposite sides of the center of mass (x). This diagram, not to scale, shows how Nemesis -- if it exists -- might orbit the Sun.

When the two stars are at their greatest separation ...

... and at their closest

SUN

NEMESIS

How Far is Far?

Nemesis is predicted to range from 1 to 3 light-years (ly) from the Sun. Shown also is the nearest known star, Proxima Centauri. On this scale, distant Pluto is too close to be marked.

PROXIMA CENTAURI

| SUN | 1 LY | NEMESIS | 3 LY | 4.25 LY |

ROBERT ROY BRITT / SPACE.COM   SOURCES: RICHARD A. MULLER; UNIVERSE, BY KAUFMANN & FREEDMAN

Nemesis is a hypothetical, hard-to-see red dwarf star or brown dwarf, orbiting the Sun at a distance of about 50,000 to 100,000 AU (about 1-2 light years), somewhat beyond the Oort cloud. This star was originally postulated to exist as part of a hypothesis to explain a perceived cycle of mass extinctions in the geological record, which seem to occur once every 26 million years or so. In addition, observations by astronomers of the sharp edges of Port clouds around other binary (double) star systems in contrast to the diffuse edges of the Port clouds around single-star

170

systems has prompted some scientists to also postulate that a dwarf star may be co-orbiting our sun. Counter-theories also exist that other forces (like the angular effect of the galactic gravity plane) may be the cause of the sharp-edged Port cloud pattern around our own sun. To date the issue remains unsettled in the scientific community.

In 1984, paleontologists David Raup and Jack Sepkoski published a paper claiming that they had identified a statistical periodicity in extinction rates over the last 250 million years using various forms of time series analysis. They focused on the extinction intensity of fossil families of marine vertebrates, invertebrates, and protozoans, identifying 12 extinction events over the time period in question. The average time interval between extinction events was determined as 26 million years. At the time, two of the identified extinction events (Cretaceous-Tertiary and Late Eocene) could be shown to coincide with large impact events. Although Raup and Sepkoski could not identify the cause of their supposed periodicity, they suggested that there might be a non-terrestrial connection. The challenge to propose a mechanism was quickly addressed by several teams of astronomers.

Two teams of astronomers, Whitmire and Jackson, and Davis, Hut, and Muller, independently published similar hypotheses to explain Raup and Sepkoski's extinction periodicity in the same issue of the journal Nature. This hypothesis proposes that the sun may have an as yet undetected companion star in a highly elliptical orbit that periodically disturbs comets in the Ourt cloud, causing a large increase in the number of comets visiting the inner solar system with a consequential increase in impact events on Earth. This became known as the Nemesis (or, more colorfully, Death Star) hypothesis.

If it does exist, the exact nature of Nemesis is uncertain. Richard A. Muller suggests that the most likely object is a red dwarf with magnitude between 7 and 12, while Daniel P.

Whitmire and Albert A. Jackson argue for a brown dwarf. If a red dwarf, it would undoubtedly already exist in star catalogs, but its true nature would only be detectable by measuring its parallax; due to orbiting the Sun it would have a very low proper motion and would escape detection by proper motion surveys that have found stars like the 9th magnitude Barnard's star.

The last major extinction event was about 5 million years ago, so Muller posits that Nemesis is likely 1 to 1.5 light years away at present, and even has ideas of what area of the sky it might be in (supported by Yarris, 1987), near Hydra, based on a hypothetical orbit derived from original apogees of a number of atypical long-period comets that describe an orbital arc meeting the specifications of Muller's hypothesis.

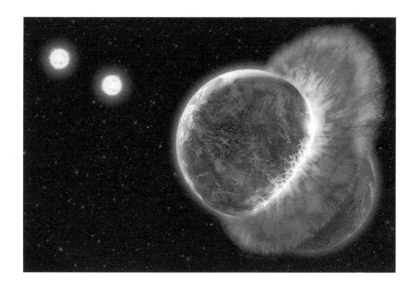

Another recent theory called "Orpheus" suggests a large body entered our solar system in the past and collided with our Earth. From that collision the debris formed into our current moon.

In 1898, George Howard Darwin made an early suggestion that the Earth and Moon had once been one body. Darwin's hypothesis was that a molten Moon had been spun from the Earth because of centrifugal forces, and this became the dominant academic explanation. Using Newtonian mechanics, he calculated that the Moon had actually orbited much closer in the past and was drifting away from the Earth. This drifting was later confirmed by American and Soviet experiments using laser ranging targets placed on the Moon.

However, Darwin's calculations could not resolve the mechanics required to trace the Moon backwards to the surface of the Earth. In 1946, Reginald Aldworth Daly of Harvard University challenged Darwin's explanation, adjusting it to postulate that the creation of the Moon was caused by an impact rather than centrifugal forces. Little attention was paid to Professor Daly's challenge until a conference on satellites in 1974 where it was reintroduced. It was then republished in Icarus in 1975 by Drs. William K. Hartmann and Donald R. Davis. Their models suggested that, at the end of the planet formation period, several satellite-sized bodies had formed that could collide with the planets or be captured. They proposed that one of these objects may have collided with the Earth, ejecting refractory, volatile-poor dust that could coalesce to form the Moon. This collision could help explain the unique geological properties of the Moon.

A similar approach was taken by Alfred G. W. Cameron and William Ward, who suggested that the Moon was formed by the tangential impact of a body the size of Mars. The outer silicates of the colliding body would mostly be vaporized, whereas a metallic core would not. Hence, most of the collisional material sent into orbit would consist of silicates, leaving the coalescing Moon deficient in iron. The more volatile materials that were emitted during the collision would likely escape the Solar System, whereas silicates would tend to coalesce.

In the last decade, we have seen a huge increase of interest from the astronomical community to the idea that a planet x does exist. There have been a flurry of press continuing reporting on new findings from independent teams claiming they may have found planet x.

Several smaller bodies have recently been found beyond Pluto. Most of them range from 800-1000km in radius. Nothing even close to the Sumerian descriptions of a planet 4-8 times the size of Earth has yet to be located and imaged using our telescopes.

How do astronomers go about looking for a planet x? And who are these people?

The most recent finding at the time of writing this comes from a Japanese team lead by Dr.

Tadashi Mukai. I contacted Dr. Mukai to ask about the size of Planet x he was projecting. He was kind enough to share this information below.

****

Dear Jason Martell-san,

Thank you for sending me information.

(Answer from Mukai) Its diameter is expected as 10,000-16,000km (roughly the same as the size of Earth). Other details for Planet x is shown in the web site at http://www.org.kobe-u.ac.jp/cps/press080228_j.html Unfortunately, most of the news in Japanese, but you can get more from PDF file in item 1).

Best regards. Tadashi Mukai

****

One of the latest space telescopes deployed is called SIRTF - space infrared telescope facility, recently rename to Spitizer. This telescope is special in that it is kept below freezing temperatures and is able to tune its infrared capability in such a way as to match the temperature of these so called "dust clouds" deep in space allowing for a never seen before clarity deep into space.

John Carr of the Naval Research Laboratory, Washington, and Joan Najita of the National

Optical Astronomy Observatory, Tucson, Arizona, developed a new technique using Spitzer's infrared spectrograph to measure and analyze the chemical composition of the gases within protoplanetary disks. These are flattened disks of gas and dust that encircle young stars. Scientists believe they provide the building materials for planets and moons and eventually, over millions of years, evolve into orbiting planetary systems like our own.

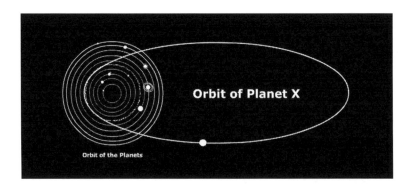

Ancient Planet X – Nibiru – Planet of the Crossing

In the early 1990's, calculations by the United States Naval Observatory have confirmed the orbital perturbation exhibited by Uranus and

Neptune, which Dr. Thomas C Van Flandern, an astronomer at the observatory, says could be explained by "a single undiscovered planet." He and a colleague, Dr. Robert Harrington, calculate that the tenth planet should be two to five times more massive than Earth and have a highly elliptical orbit that takes it some 5 billion miles beyond that of Pluto.

We know today that beyond the giant planets Jupiter and Saturn lie more major planets, Uranus and Neptune, and a small planet, Pluto. But such knowledge is quite recent. Uranus was discovered, through the use of improved telescopes, in 1781. Neptune was pinpointed by astronomers (guided by mathematical calculations) in 1846. It became evident that Neptune was being subjected to an unknown gravitational pull, and in 1930 Pluto (was located). The latest advances in space imaging do not rely solely on orbital perturbations as the way for locating and identifying possible candidates for Planet x.

The 6,000 year old Sumerian descriptions of our solar system include one more planet they called "Nibiru," which means "Planet of the crossing." The descriptions of this planet by the Sumerians match precisely the specifications of "planet x" (the Tenth Planet), which is currently being sought by astronomers in the depths of our own Solar System. Why has Planet x not been seen in recent times? Views from modern and ancient astronomy, which both suggest a highly elliptical, comet-like orbit, takes Planet x into the depths of space, well beyond the orbit of Pluto. We discovered Pluto with our telescopes just recently in 1930. Is it not possible that there are other forces at work on our solar system besides the nine planets we know of? Sumerian descriptions of Our Solar System are being confirmed with modern advances in science.

Pangea Explained By The Sumerians

To illustrate some of the amazing knowledge the Sumerians possessed 6,000 years ago, I will use a reference to something that to this day is still being taught by our education system. When the Earth was much older, we can determine the land mass was once a clumped together mass at one point in time. But due to the process known as "Continental Drift" or "Plate tectonics," the land clump was slowly pulled apart to where the current land masses are today.

We can see clear proof that the continents were all once connected by simply looking at a map of the Earth and seeing how the pieces fit. That would only mean that at one time, Earth was basically half a planet.

Where did the other half go? Why is Earth only half a planet? The diagrams shown here are descriptions from the Sumerians explaining how our Earth came to be... They state that the satellites of Planet x (Nibiru) as they called it, collided with our primitive Earth in the past. Creating the asteroid belt and forever becoming another member of our solar system in a comet like 3,600 year orbit around the sun.

In February, 1971, the United States launched Pioneer 10. Pioneer 10 scientists attached to it an engraved aluminum plaque. It attempts to tell whoever might find the plaque that Mankind is male and female, etc., and that (Pioneer 10) is from the 3rd planet of this Sun. Our astronomy is geared to the notion that Earth is the 3rd planet, which indeed it is if one begins the count from the center of our system, the Sun. But to someone nearing our solar system from the outside, the 1st planet to be encountered would be Pluto, the second Neptune, the 3rd Uranus, the 4th Saturn, the 5th Jupiter, the 6th Mars .. and the Earth would be 7th.

The (12th) Planet's periodic appearance and disappearance from Earth's view confirms the assumption of its permanence in solar orbit.

The Mesopotamian texts spoke of the planet's periodic appearance as an anticipated, predictable, and observable event. The nearing planet, however, was expected to cause rains and flooding, as its strong gravitational effects have been known to do. Like the Mesopotamian savants, the Hebrew prophets considered the time of the planet's approaching Earth and becoming visible to Mankind as ushering in a new era.

Wherever the archaeologists uncovered the remains of Near Eastern peoples, the symbol of the Winged Disk was conspicuous, dominating temples and palaces, carved on rocks, etched on cylinder seals and painted on walls. It accompanied kings and priests, stood above their thrones, "hovered" above them in battle scenes, and was etched into their chariots.

Central to the religious beliefs and astronomy of the ancient world remained within the solar system and that its grand orbit returned it periodically to the Earth's vicinity. The pictograph sign for the 12th planet the "Planet of the Crossing," was a cross.

The ancient peoples not only expected the periodic arrival of the 12th planet, but also charted its advancing course. Many of the Sumerian Cylinder seals describe a planet whose orbit takes it far beyond Pluto, but also comes in from the SOUTH and moves in a clockwise direction - according to the Mesopotamian data.

The most intriguing part of this information is that if we do confirm the existence of Planet x, we may very well have ancestors that live on this planet. All the religious texts that speak of beings coming down from the heavens would be put into a new light of understanding. Many of the myths from ancient cultures might just turn out to be facts we confirm in the near future.

The Lost Cycle of Time

I opened this book by talking about an apocalypse—a veil to be lifted. We have discussed many ways in which conventional, mainstream ways of looking at history, archeology and science keep us from seeing the underlying truth. We are still not finished. Our distant ancestors have left yet another message for us, echoing down through the ages, and this one can be uncovered in the realm of astronomy. This knowledge may lead us to realize our present potential as humans on this Earth and, in a sense, rediscover that which we have lost over the years.

I have mentioned the precession of the equinox throughout this book, mostly in reference to how so many megalithic structures across the Earth were clearly designed to measure or mirror it. Let me take a moment now to explain what is meant by the precession of the equinox, how it is traditionally defined and measured, and then to uncover some other information about it that has recently come to light.

The precession of the equinox can be seen as the rate at which the stars move across the night sky from our perspective, relative to Earth's equinox. Now, typically mainstream science purports that this precession is the result of the gravity of our Sun and Moon causing Earth's axis to wobble. This is known as the Lunisolar
Theory, for obvious reasons. However, the Binary Research Institute has recently begun to offer an alternative explanation, known as the Binary Theory or Binary Model. Let me explain how this theory differs.

The Binary Theory suggests that most of the observable aspects of the precession are actually due to the motion of the solar system, which curves gradually through space, relative to the fixed stars. It has recently been discovered that this theory offers a superior explanation for how the precession rate accelerates, and it also offers a better way to predict how the precession rate changes. Basically, this theory answers many of the questions that the Lunisolar

Theory has failed to answer and it resolves several inconsistencies of the older theory.

Before we dive more deeply into a comparison of these theories and why it is relevant to our overall discussion in this book, let's look in a bit more detail at some of the celestial motions that have an important effect on our lives on the Earth. The first is called diurnal motion, or the Earth's rotation on its axis. This motion is what brings us from a waking to a sleeping state every day. We are so used to this process happening subtly and naturally because we are in tune with the Earth's rotation. Thus these daily changes in our consciousness occur practically without our notice. This is the way in which our bodies are attuned to the motion of the planet.

The second celestial motion that we have to look at is the Earth's movement around the Sun—first described, as we know, by Copernicus. This movement around our sun is the celestial motion that causes life to bloom and grow on our planet, as well as affecting how it decomposes, moves, or disappears. The Earth's movement around the Sun is responsible in large part for the evolution and adaptation patterns of the trillions of species that exist on this planet. It is so relevant to human life that we cannot fail to notice it each day, and to be almost constantly aware of it. The way in which this motion takes place, like diurnal motion, is essentially undisputed.

The third celestial motion, however, is still the product of much dispute. This is the relevant one we will be discussing in more detail here —it is the precession of the equinox. As I mentioned above, there are conflicting theories on how this precession occurs. That is, we all can observe that, day by day—(or night by night, if you will)— the way in which the stars appear in the sky subtly shifts. This motion is not always considered to be as immediately relevant to human life as, of course, the Earth's rotation on its axis and its revolution around the sun. It is, however, incredibly significant, as we can see from any examination of ancient cultures. And, as I have discussed with Stonehenge, Maccu Piccu, the Egyptian Pyramids and various other megalithic structures around the Earth, this precession of the equinox has been measured and observed with great significance by many ancient cultures. It is to the past that we must now turn to understand the importance of this.

The amount of time that it takes for the precession to be dramatically apparent is what makes it more difficult to notice its significance. The precessional cycle is roughly 24,000 years in total. Well, naturally, with our human life expectancy of a mere 80 years or so, we only live to see a tiny, tiny shred of the precession happen. We believe what we can see, so of course it is easy to overlook the importance of something that takes place so slowly as to be almost imperceptible. However, we must not overlook it anymore. This precession is related to a higher state of consciousness that as humans we have the possibility to achieve, if only we look to our ancestors and learn how. Perhaps there was some type of golden age in the past, and perhaps we have the potential to see one again—or at least to recognize our true place in the cycle of time.

In their famous book, "Hamlet's Mill," Giorgio de Santillana and Hertha von Dechend explore the folk stories and mythologies of thirty ancient cultures, and what their study reveals is remarkable. It appears that all of these ancient peoples—and who knows how many others?—believed in a very different model of history than that which predominates our modern age of so-called rationality. Essentially, the difference is that in these ancient cosmologies, both human consciousness and the motion of history were viewed as cyclical rather than linear. These ancient cultural beliefs are very tied in with the precession of the equinox. It was widely believed that time moves in a great cycle corresponding to the precession of the equinox, and that within this cycle exists an alternating pattern of Dark Ages and Golden

Ages. The philosopher Plato viewed this cycle as what he called the Great Year.

In our contemporary world, steeped in the Judeo-Christian tradition, this concept of a vast cycle—connected to the almost imperceptible, gradual precession of the equinox—is somewhat strange. However, in the pre-Christian world, it is quite clear that this idea was extremely common. It was certainly not viewed as fantasy, but as solid fact by a great number of cultures across the Earth. It is now becoming clear, due to recent discoveries in astronomy, that this idea of a Golden Age is much more than a story. There is a great deal of evidence now coming to light that backs this concept scientifically, in both the realm of astronomy as well as archeology.

Not only might Plato's idea of the Great Year be based in verifiable scientific fact, but if so then the whole idea of the 2012 ending of the Mayan Calendar may have much more importance than many believe. The most important element of figuring out how all this works is to look closely at the precession of the equinox, for this is where the heart of the mystery lies.

Just as we can easily observe the Earth's rotation by observing the sun rising in the east and setting in the west each day, so can we also observe a similar pattern in the stars on a yearly basis, rather than a daily basis. That is, as we move through a year's time, the stars "rise" in the eastern sky and "set" in the western sky. As this is taking place, the constellations of the zodiac—of which there are twelve—move through the sky in such a way that one per month is visible. Hence, we associate one constellation for each of the twelve months of the year.

But let's say we just looked at the sky once a year on a given day—an equinox, for example. We would then observe that the stars move retrograde—or opposite to the Earth's rotation and revolution—at a very slow rate indeed. This rate is approximately one degree every seventy years. This means that the equinox will fall on a different constellation once in every 2,000 years. That means it takes about 24,000 years to finish its cycle through the twelve constellations, or signs of the zodiac. This movement—which is essentially a slow, subtle and steady backward motion—is what we know as the precession of the equinox. The Latin prefix "pre," of course, reminds us of the direction of this motion—before, backwards in relation to the fixed stars.

How exactly this process works, as I mentioned at the beginning of this section, is the subject of opposing theories. How does the Earth change its orientation to unmoving space in this slow and steady, observable way? There is, of course, one predominant theory generally accepted by mainstream science. This standard explanation—the Lunisolar Theory—purports that the gravity of the Moon is acting upon the oblate sphere of the Earth, slowly and steadily throughout the year. This theory is based, however, upon an understanding of the solar system that presumes a fixed solar system. But what if the solar system is not entirely fixed in space? What if it does, itself, move through space? Consistent with this dynamical theory, researchers at the Binary Research Institute have recently created a model of our solar system that moves. This model offers a remarkable possibility for observing the precession. It also, interestingly, seems to resolve several other anomalies that the traditional Lunisolar Theory does not explain.

According to ancient astronomy, the precession of the equinox—the slow movement of the zodiac's constellations—is the result of the sun's motion. Basically, this understanding describes the sun as curving through space around some other star, and this means that our viewpoint of the stars from here on Earth changes. So, it is our viewpoint of the stars that is actually changing rather than the position of the Earth relative to the stars, as the traditional theory suggest. Top research astronomers are now actually scientifically proving this ancient dynamic model. Although the Sun's companion star has not yet been identified, this Binary Theory of the precession is rapidly emerging as the most plausible.

What's so remarkable about this is that, in fact, this is not a new theory—it is a very, very old theory indeed. Think back to Plato describing a Great Year, and all of the ancient cultures explored in "Hamlet's Mill" that spoke of this alternative view of time.

To explain this dynamic model of the precession a bit more clearly, let's say that the Earth is carried by the solar system as we know it. This solar system, rather than staying put in space, is actually moving in a massive orbit, bringing Earth along with it. This causes our planet to be subjected to the electromagnetic spectrum of another star (besides our own known Sun) along the solar system's orbit. Naturally, this would have a profound impact on our magnetosphere, our ionosphere—in fact, all life on the planet. We already know that the diurnal motion (Earth's rotation on its axis) and the annual motion (Earth's revolution around the Sun) are responsible for the transitions from day to night and through the seasons of the year. These motions are directly produced as a result of the Earth's changing position relative to the EM spectrum of the Sun.

Let me ask you this. If these two commonly understood motions of the Earth have such a profound effect on our perception of time, on life in general—and not just human life, but in fact all life on this planet—what do you think might be the effect of an even grander type of celestial motion? What the Binary Theory offers us is an opportunity to understand life on a radically grander scale. It offers us a way to understand how human consciousness relates to the celestial cycles—and how Plato's concept of the Great Year might be much more than theory. If we consider the idea that the entire solar system is moving constantly and gradually, then we must also consider the possibility of Golden and Dark Ages on a vast scale.

Turning to some current research on the effect of the bigger celestial motion at play upon human consciousness, we can look at some of the findings of Dr. Valerie Hunt. An expert in human physiology, Dr. Hunt has conducted numerous studies related to human cognition and the electromagnetic field. The ambient EM field surrounds us all the time and it can have a profound effect on human consciousness and cognition. What is most remarkable about this research is that it has been shown that human consciousness is notably affected by very small changes in light. The Great Year or Cycle of Time theory of human history is based upon the Sun's movement through space and how this movement subjects Earth to shifting stellar fields. So, depending upon the amount and quality of the EM spectra we are receiving, human consciousness—the way we think and even how well we think—may be profoundly affected in different eras of time. Doesn't this make sense if we think about how differently historical periods have affected us? Wouldn't this go a long way toward explaining the phenomena of changing attitudes and beliefs across cultures and through human history as we look at the different eras of our life on this planet? Wouldn't it help to explain why some ages are Golden and others Dark?

To sum up: celestial motion on a grand scale as explained by the Binary Model=profound shifts in human consciousness from era to era.

As anyone familiar with a mainstream historical perspective knows, the mythologies and stories of the ancient cultures throughout time are usually dismissed as just that—stories. Fairytales. Contemporary western culture ignores on a grand scale any suggestion that there might be some kind of larger, external force at work on the human consciousness. Such ideas are usually associated with, if anything, questions of faith or religion. But I am not talking about faith or religion. I am talking about scientific fact.

As we know, mainstream scientific theory embraces a linear model of human development that moves from the primitive to the modern on a straight trajectory. We are told that humans were primitive, hunter-gatherers up until the last 5,000 years or so. Then, tribal societies began to emerge— mostly of necessity as different groups began to make war upon each other. We are told that there we no largely populated civilizations until after written communication was developed. Similarly, we are led to believe that these primitive societies of old had no complex engineering systems or structures until after the development of writing.

From our study of the megalithic structures all over the Earth earlier in this book, we know that this is simply not true. What about the complex idols of Easter Island and no evidence of how this was achieved in writing? What about the megaliths in South America such as on the Nazca plain? In recent years, it is becoming more and more clear all the time that these anomalies cannot be resolved. In this short book alone, I have covered several discoveries from ancient cultures that utterly challenge the idea that advanced human development is a recent thing.

Clearly, we can see that many ancient civilizations had knowledge of things that would be inconsistent with the age in which they lived. There are so many anomalies that have been discovered throughout South America, Asia, the Middle East, Europe—all over the world. We have already talked about the Annunaki—the race of alien beings from planet x who, in all likelihood, are our ancestors. They imparted to us wondrous abilities to construct things and to use technology, advance mathematics and architecture.

ORINST. P 24975 PERSEPOLIS, IRAN
COUNCIL HALL. AHURAMAZDA SYMBOL
ON THE NORTH JAMB OF THE EASTERN
DOORWAY OF THE MAIN HALL.

C12

My discussion here of the Annunaki challenges mainstream science, but it happens to be underscored by cold, hard scientific fact if you open your eyes to them. It is the same with the Lost Cycle of Time, which we must begin opening our eyes to in order to see our real place in the universe and our relationship to the passing of time.

As we have discussed in detail, it is probable that time does not in fact simply move in a linear pattern, although we are so used to thinking of it this way. We must accept that it is a cycle, and that we are simply existing now in one phase of that cycle. But it is not a trajectory from less advanced to more advanced. Rather, it cycles back and forth over a 24,000 year period from Golden Ages to Dark Ages.

If you think about Egypt for a moment, you know that the famous pyramids are some of the most impressive structures on Earth. Recently, pyramids have been discovered in Peru and dated at 2700 BC. Incidentally, this matches with the Egyptian pyramids and other megalithic structures that have been found in Mesopotamia. Even though the Peruvian pyramids lie across an ocean from Egypt, the technology used in both cases is similar—and utterly baffling.

We are generally taught that the development of a written language and the construction of weapons are signs of what could be considered a civilized culture. However, in neither of these locations do we discover either of these things. We do see other remarkable signs of advanced human civilization, however. Perhaps all of those years ago, we were in a Golden Age?

So much evidence is emerging to challenge the traditional theory of time that we simply cannot ignore it. In this book alone, we have already covered so many technological and archeological enigmas it boggles the mind.

We cannot fail to notice also that in so many cases, the advanced civilizations responsible for these enigmas suddenly, rapidly declined or completely disappeared from their region of the Earth. In many cases, they disappeared all at once—leaving absolutely no sign of what caused their demise. How can so many civilized cultures of antiquity be so shrouded in mystery? Why did so many advance peoples suddenly cease to exist or to decline slowly and steadily over a period of years?

If we look at the period of the Dark Ages that we commonly refer to in our typical perspective of historic time, we know that all the brilliant thriving civilizations I have discussed throughout this book were gone by this period. They had either disappeared or for one reason or another left their lands and become nomads. That's why we call them the Dark Ages. In many cases, even the indigenous populations of these regions who live there today knew nothing of their predecessors just a few years after. Think of the indigenous people of South America, who cannot explain the wonders of Puma Punku or Maccu Picchu any better than you or I.

These civilizations disappeared at the Cycle of Time turned. We can call it a cyclic downturn, and I leave it to you to question whether we are still in this period or have emerged from it. This downturn was characterized by the disappearance of advanced technologies, the spread of disease and illiteracy, and declining knowledge of mathematics and science.

How does this relate to the Binary Theory of the precession? What we see if we look at the facts is evidence that human consciousness underwent a massive change. Knowledge and skills we once possessed vanished into thin air. It's as if our species forgot or lost its capabilities to perform certain tasks. It's as if all at once, our species went back in time. If we think of Dr. Hunt's findings that I mentioned earlier, we can clearly see that human consciousness as a whole can collectively be affected, and this would explain these radical and sudden shifts in human history.

Naturally, it is hard to find records of the precise moment in time when this shift occurred, but we do have some visual evidence in the form of ancient Mithraic bas-reliefs. These portray two boys atop a scene depicting the slaying of the bull (Taurus), and they are standing on each side of the zodiac. One of the boys holds a torch ascending one side of the zodiac symbol—designating a period of light and illumination. On the other side, the other boy points his torch downward into the darkness—clearly suggesting decline, darkness.

We can look at the following chart to see how these images of light and darkness correspond to the epochs of the Earth. According to the Greeks, we are moving slowly through these various epochs of higher consciousness—and declining consciousness.

Many historians put forth theories regarding which civilizations succeed versus those that fail based on environmental or geographic differences. That is, it is often suggested that those civilizations who devise the best methods of warfare or protection, or who have the least exposure to disease are the ones who survive. The decline of certain civilizations based on this model can then be explained by their lacks in these areas. These theories are certainly applicable to much that has gone on over the last several thousand years, but they do nothing to explain larger trends that we can observe across all cultures.

Basically, we must consider the idea that it is not just Earth's environment that affects us and has affected civilizations of the past. If we allow the possibility of the Great Year theory, we can include the motion (environment, if you will) of the solar system on the whole. We can bring in the impact of celestial motion to explain these dramatic, previously unexplained changes. Just as we move through the four seasons of the year, so is our solar system on the whole pulling us through a 24,000 year Great Year. In it, we also have seasons—only these seasons are of rising and falling human consciousness, and they each last approximately 6,000 years.

This idea of rising and falling human consciousness based on the motion of the solar system contextualizes so many seemingly mysterious ancient mythologies. It offers an understanding of how anomalous devices like the Babylon battery came into being. This concept radically broadens our understanding of how so many enigmas came to be and gives us a better understanding of our place in the Universe.

Where are we now in the Cycle of Time?

To answer this question, we can look to the past—to the words of ancient historians as well as ancient myths. According to some Native American folklore, there are cities at the bottom of the sea that were built during the last Golden Age. Hesiod of ancient Greece tells us of a time long past when "peace and plenty" ruled the Earth.

Just as we now break the seasons of the year into four—autumn, winter, spring and summer —it is also common to see the eras of the Great Year broken into four. Vedic scriptures describe four eons or yugas known as Kali, Dwapara, Treta and Satya, with the Satya yuga being a golden era. Ancient Mayans numbered a series of worlds and suns to identify each era. The language we are perhaps most familiar with would be the terminology used by the ancient Greeks, who describe The Iron Age, The Bronze Age, the Silver Age and of course the Golden Age.

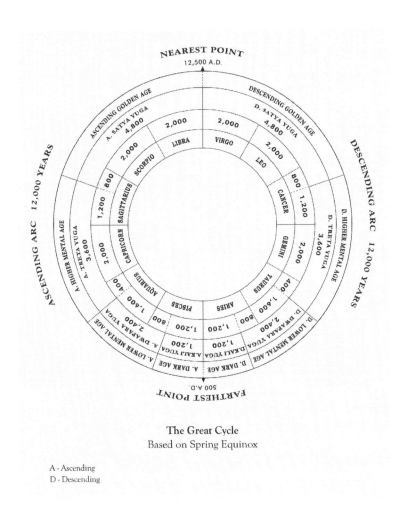

The Great Cycle
Based on Spring Equinox

A - Ascending
D - Descending

However the eras are labeled, they follow the same pattern. Essentially, it comes down to this: our consciousness as humans is at its lowest point whenever our solar system moves the farthest from our Sun's companion star. Conversely, our consciousness is the

216

most elevated when we are at our closest point to that same star. The last time we were at the lowest point was in 500 AD—makes sense, right? And the next time we will reach a Golden Age will be in 12,500 AD. Looking at the zodiac, we can locate these points where the autumnal equinox sun intersects with one of the 12 constellations. Typically, Aries is located at the 12 o'clock point of the zodiac, and when our autumnal equinox sun reaches this place, Earth is experiencing its optimal stellar environment. Many people at this point will achieve an elevated state of consciousness. However, when this autumnal equinox sun is located in Libra, we find the opposite is the case. At such times, a weak or deluded consciousness dominates.

Right now, we find ourselves in an ascending age, moving from the Iron Age (also called the Age of Man) into the Bronze Age (or Age of the Hero). Clearly, we are a long way from the Ages of Silver and Bronze—also called the Age of the Demigods and the Age of the Gods, respectively.

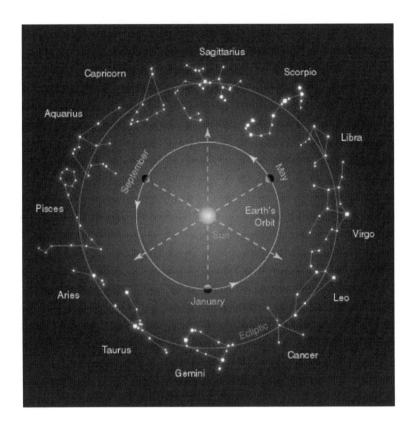

If we keep the big picture in mind, we can make a number of interesting correlations. At the present time we are engaged in a slow but steady period of awakening consciousness. We are emerging from a period in which our consciousness was perceived as purely physical, merely an aspect or inhabitant of the body. We are beginning to see that, in fact, we are made up of energy, not just purely tangible matter. We can see this movement in our consciousness evolution if we look to the discovery of electricity and the laws of gravity, as well as the development of observational instruments like microscopes and telescopes. In fact, much of this ascending shift can be traced to the Renaissance and we observe a steady progression through the following historical periods, particularly once we get to the discoveries of Albert Einstein and the development of quantum physics.

Essentially, we are beginning to be aware of ourselves as energetic beings connected to the energy that makes up the universe. In many ways, the veils that lie between our consciousness and all the vastness of the universe are becoming thinner and thinner—being lifted. Many people even now assert that as this shift continues, we will move into a time period when telepathy and psychic abilities become common place—elements of an expanded human consciousness.

There is already a great deal of mythology and folklore across the cultures that speak of a time in the past when these things were commonplace. This time is said to have taken place around 3100 BC, according to Vedic scripture. If you look at the Judeo-Christian Bible, Genesis describes a time when humanity was at one with nature—before the Age of Babel when God confused the tongues. Evidence of a more permeable relationship between the individual consciousness and the core energies of the universe is found is all our human stories. Whether you dismiss them as mere fairytales or science fiction, you cannot ignore their presence everywhere. Perhaps it is not so much a matter of developing or cultivating our abilities, as it is a matter of remembering them.

A mere five hundred years ago, poverty, war, ignorance and disease swept through large populations on this planet and destroyed them. Human rights and social equality were unexplored concepts; the human lifespan was brutally short. Today, of course, we still suffer from wars and disease—it is far from a Golden Age yet. But still, there is a movement happening, a growing number of people who believe that they have a profound connection to the Universe on the whole. Consciousness is already shifting and expanding.

The more we are willing explore and to accept the reality of our past as a species on this planet, the more bravely we can move forward into our future. We cannot do this blindly. We must pull the veil from our eyes and accept what we see.

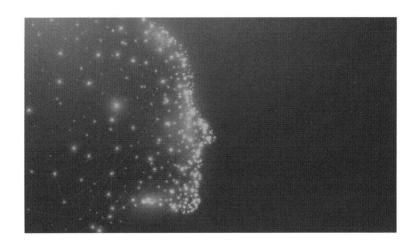

Aliens & AI

We have all seen the movies (2010, Terminator, iRobot, Red Planet, etc) Where "A.I." is going to stop listening to us, and rebel to destroy humanity.

But instead we should come to realize the potential A.I. has to help assist us in the efforts of Ufology.

First off, please be aware you are already using A.I. everyday in your life when you talk to Google, Siri, Cortana etc through your mobile device.

A.I. is moving into other forms like robot assistants that can interact with our pets and kids to teach and entertain them. We should accept that soon we will also have almost life-like androids within our culture.

What is interesting to note, from the Ufology point of view is we have seen throughout time the use of A.I. from intelligent beings visiting earth.

If we go all the way back to Sumerian times, in 3,600 B.C. we find figurine statues of beings they called the IGGI. These beings are written about in ancient Sumerian texts as being helpers of the gods. They assisted in medical experiments, helped fly and navigate their craft. There were texts that wrote about the IGIG where you could ask them a set of questions to determine if they were alive or just acting as so.

This really begs the question if the IGIG are in fact a hybrid / android race of beings used as assistants for the upper gods in ancient times called the Annunaki.

Even in modern UFO sightings, there is often a smaller ball of light or other object that accompanies the craft. Remember the scene in Close Encounters as the UFO's fly around the street corner only to be followed by a mysterious red ball of light.

Using Close Encounter to further the reference to A.I. - if you remember the scene when the main UFO mothership lands to begin communicating with the gourd team they use audio tones to find a baseline of communication.

But the mothership needs to communicate at a much higher pace in order to have a meaningful exchange. So we turn on our A.I. and the audio conversation gets taken over by a computer to interact on our behalf with the mothership.

It's at this point that a meaningful exchange of conversation takes place allowing for a baseline of understanding which sounds like they are communicating tones across the spectrum from caution to joy :)

After this tonal vocabulary is established, It's at that point the aliens come out and interact with us. Returning the humans that left 30 years ago, and taking aboard a new batch of participants that will leave in the mothership.

More current movies like "The Arrival" also do a good job of showing us how we could hypothetically use A.I. to communicate with aliens.

In that movie the aliens use a language that goes beyond time and can predict the future. But we have no way to understand all the symbols and their meaning. So we build an A.I. machine learning system which the main actors accessed via a laptop.

When the aliens would speak in their usual language, the A.I. would find those symbols in a stored database and display the best guess for the meaning of those words. This allows for a baseline of communication between us and the aliens.

Imagine how A.I. could have been used in the work from the late Clifford Stone who claimed to be dispatched by the military to investigate crashed UFO incidents.

They would be faced with a problem of how to communicate with the aliens and would benefit from the use A.I. that learns a basic cross pattern of reference for a baseline we can both use to communicate.

We should look to develop more tools using off-the-shelf API's for A.I. (Google, Amazon) to train machine learning and look for UFO's, UAP's, and other phenomena.

Mars 2026 Prediction

We are scheduled to send a manned mission to Mars in 2026 with a long term goal of a permanent settlement on Mars.
Once we have established a base on Mars, and begin exploring the planet "feet to ground" there will be some amazing opportunities to finally confirm just how far

back human civilization really goes. The cydonia region of Mars probably contains many artifacts beyond the obvious huge megaliths in the form of an ancient city built right on a shoreline with a huge human / lion-like face staring up into space.

We might find actual humans remains or even non-human remains that clearly show we both occupied Mars in the past.

The real question is who is still there today? There have been rumors for many years that the US, Israel, Russia - all have bases on the Moon and Mars and have been there for 25 years. The question as to why we have not visited the Moon or Mars publicly can only be answered by the fact this is an aliens presence they are shrouding from the public. Maybe this information is finally going to come out if we are being given access to the Moon and Mars. Are we ready to meet the ancient gods?

The Current UAP/UFO Cover-Up

For over half a century, the veil of secrecy surrounding unidentified aerial phenomena (UAP) and unidentified flying objects (UFOs) has been meticulously maintained. The evidence, often obscured and dismissed by official channels, reveals a consistent pattern of obfuscation and deceit. This chapter delves into the mechanisms of this cover-up, examining the intricate web of disinformation and the compelling testimonies that point to a hidden truth.

The Long Road of Deception: Project Blue Book, The Condon Report, and ATIP

The story of the UAP/UFO cover-up begins with a series of government-sanctioned investigations that were ostensibly aimed at uncovering the truth. Project Blue Book, initiated in 1952, was one of the first major efforts by the United States Air Force to investigate UFO sightings. However, despite cataloging over 12,000 sightings, the project concluded with a report that largely dismissed the phenomenon as natural or man-made occurrences. This conclusion, many believe, was a deliberate attempt to mislead the public and maintain the status quo.

Following Blue Book, the Condon Report of the late 1960s further entrenched the narrative of skepticism. Commissioned by the United States Air Force and conducted by physicist Edward Condon, the report declared that there was no compelling evidence to support the existence of extraterrestrial phenomena. Yet, critics argue that the Condon Report was biased from the outset, designed to quell public interest rather than explore the evidence objectively.

The Advanced Aerospace Threat Identification Program (AATIP), operational from 2007 to 2012, represents a more recent example of the ongoing cover-up. Despite its mandate to investigate UAPs, AATIP's findings were shrouded in secrecy, and the program itself was kept under wraps until 2017. These initiatives, spanning decades, share a common goal: to mislead the public and stifle genuine disclosure.

A Hidden Space Program: The Shadow NASA

Beyond these public-facing programs lies a more insidious layer of secrecy. There is compelling evidence to suggest the existence of a covert space program, often referred to as the "Shadow NASA." This clandestine operation, reportedly active for over 50 years, is believed to involve a fleet of advanced spacecraft controlled by the United States Navy. Unlike the public NASA, which operates under the scrutiny of media and government oversight, the Shadow NASA functions in complete secrecy, its activities hidden from the public eye.

The existence of this secret space program aligns with numerous reports and testimonies from credible sources. For instance, Sergeant Clifford Stone, a former United States Army officer, has publicly stated that he was involved in crash retrieval operations and had direct knowledge of extraterrestrial beings.

Similarly, Colonel Philip J. Corso, in his book "The Day After Roswell," detailed his involvement in the recovery of alien technology, which he claimed was subsequently reverse-engineered and integrated into modern military applications.

Face-to-Face Encounters: Testimonies and Evidence

Perhaps the most compelling evidence of a cover-up comes from the testimonies of those who have had direct encounters with extraterrestrial beings. Sergeant Clifford Stone's revelations are just the tip of the iceberg. The late Phil Schneider, a geologist and engineer who worked on secret government projects, claimed to have had multiple confrontations with extraterrestrials. His accounts, though controversial, have garnered a significant following among those who believe in the existence of a hidden extraterrestrial presence on Earth.

Another significant event is the alleged meeting between extraterrestrials and U.S. officials at Holloman Air Force Base in the 1970s. This incident, shrouded in mystery and speculation, is said to involve a face-to-face encounter with beings from another world. Such encounters, if true, represent a profound aspect of the cover-up: the active engagement with extraterrestrial intelligences while keeping the public in the dark.

The Road Ahead: Disclosure and Vigilance

Despite the extensive efforts to conceal the truth, the push for disclosure continues. The proliferation of evidence and the growing number of credible witnesses make it increasingly difficult for the cover-up to persist indefinitely. Shows like "Ancient Aliens" and dedicated researchers play a crucial role in keeping the public informed and encouraging vigilance. The skies, as ever, hold the key to unveiling the secrets that have been kept for too long.

In conclusion, the ongoing UAP/UFO cover-up is a testament to the lengths to which authorities will go to maintain control over information and technology that could fundamentally alter our understanding of the universe. As more evidence comes to light, the call for transparency grows louder. The truth, it seems, is out there, waiting to be revealed.

Stay tuned to "Ancient Aliens," and keep watching the skies.

References

I'd like to thank the work of the authors below who have gone to great lengths in doing their part to bring light upon this research.

Zecharia Sitchin (1961)
The 12th Planet. HarperCollins

Erik Von Daniken (1970)
Chariots of the Gods. Berkley Books

Lloyd Pye (1998)
Everything You Know is Wrong, Adamu Press

Graham Hancock (1996)
Fingerprints of the Gods, Three Rivers Press

David Hatcher Childress (May 2000)
Technology of the Gods, Adventures Unlimited Press

Walter Cruttenden (Sept 2005)
The Lost Star, St. Lynn's Press